RULES OF THUMB
FOR BUSINESS WRITERS

Also by Jay Silverman, Elaine Hughes, and Diana Roberts Wienbroer:

Rules of Thumb: A Guide for Writers, 4th ed.
Good Measures: A Practice Book to Accompany Rules of Thumb, 4th ed.
Rules of Thumb for Research

By Diana Roberts Wienbroer:

The McGraw-Hill Guide to Electronic Research

By Elaine Hughes:

Writing from the Inner Self

By Elaine Hughes, Jay Silverman, and Diana Roberts Wienbroer:

Finding Answers: A Guide to Conducting and Reporting Research

RULES OF THUMB
FOR BUSINESS WRITERS

DIANA ROBERTS WIENBROER

ELAINE HUGHES

JAY SILVERMAN

MCGRAW-HILL

New York   San Francisco   Washington, D.C.   Auckland   Bogotá
Caracas   Lisbon   London   Madrid   Mexico City   Milan
Montreal   New Delhi   San Juan   Singapore
Sydney   Tokyo   Toronto

Library of Congress Catalog Card No.: 99-074660

McGraw-Hill

*A Division of The **McGraw·Hill** Companies*

2 3 4 5 6 7 8 9 0 DOC/DOC   0 9 8 7 6 5 4 3 2 1 0   (College)
  4 5 6 7 8 9 0 DOC/DOC   0 9 8 7 6 5 4 3 2   (Professional)

ISBN 0-07-234746-5 (College)
ISBN 0-07-135721-1 (Professional)

It was set in Palatino by North Market Street Graphics.
Printed and bound by R. R. Donnelley & Sons Company.

McGraw-Hill books are available at special quantity discounts to use as premiums and sales promotions, or for use in corporate training programs. For more information, please write to the Director of Special Sales, McGraw-Hill, Professional Publishing, Two Penn Plaza, New York, NY 10121-2298. Or contact your local bookstore.

TO OUR READERS—

WE WROTE THIS BOOK WITH YOU IN MIND
AND HOPE EVERY PAGE SERVES YOU WELL.

CONTENTS

PART FOUR: SPECIAL PROJECTS

PART FIVE: CORRECTNESS—USAGE

PART SIX: CORRECTNESS—PUNCTUATION

Acknowledgments

Many friends and colleagues have contributed to this book.

First, we wish to thank Betsy Brown, our editor at McGraw-Hill's Professional Book Group, and Lisa Moore, our editor at McGraw-Hill's College Division. We have enjoyed a long-term and supportive relationship with Betsy Brown. She and her colleagues have helped us in a number of ways to shape the image of the book. Lisa Moore and Phil Butcher, Editorial Director, at the McGraw-Hill College Division made the textbook a reality, and we are very grateful. The skill and creativity of Tom Laughman and his colleagues at North Market Street Graphics improved our manuscript immensely. Their professionalism under a very tight deadline made all the difference.

Rules of Thumb for Business Writers was written in response to friends in the business world who encouraged us to adapt our college textbook, *Rules of Thumb: A Guide for Writers,* for a larger professional audience. Over the years, their suggestions and questions shaped the concept of this book. In particular, we benefited from the advice of Russell Bosworth, Evelyn Brooks, Joylene Carlson, and Carolyn Roughsedge.

A number of colleagues have thoughtfully reviewed *Rules of Thumb for Business Writers:* Anne Gervasi, North Lake College; Gary Christenson, Elgin Community College; Robert Cason, University of Texas at El Paso; Rebecca Fraser, Nassau Community College; Rebecca Jackson, University of Illinois at Urbana-Champaign; Caryl Lynn Segal, University of Texas at Arlington; and professional writers Jerry Hill and Gordon Tappar. Our gratitude goes to each of them for careful attention to every aspect of the book.

Finally, we want to thank our families—Beverly Jensen for many kinds of support; Carl and Kirtley Wienbroer for advice on a number of different perspectives.

Portions of *Rules of Thumb for Business Writers* have appeared in different forms in *Rules of Thumb: A Guide for Writers*, *Rules of Thumb for Research*, *The McGraw-Hill Guide to Electronic Research* (all from McGraw-Hill), and *Finding Answers: A Guide to Conducting and Reporting Research* (HarperCollins).

A Note from the Authors

The phrase "rule of thumb" refers to a handy guideline: The top part of your thumb is roughly an inch long. Sometimes you need a ruler marked in millimeters, but often you can do fine by measuring with just your thumb. Your thumb takes only a second to use, and it's always with you.

Rules of Thumb for Business Writers is the third book in a series written by the three of us. The first book, published originally in 1989 and now in the fourth edition, is *Rules of Thumb: A Guide for Writers*. *Rules of Thumb for Research* was published in the fall of 1998. We wanted to call your attention to the other books because *Rules of Thumb for Business Writers* follows the same basic concepts as our prior books. Our aim has been to create handbooks that writers can use on their own—handbooks that are brief and readable, covering the main writing problems most people have trouble with.

We've made *Rules of Thumb for Business Writers* the same sort of guide. You can use it out of order, in small doses, to find what you want when you need to solve a specific writing problem, whether in the office, on the job, or at home. We've covered most of the basic writing problems that you will face on a regular basis and have also included guidelines for writing the most common kinds of documents used in business writing.

In this book, you will find some points that have to be exactly right, and in those cases, we've given the complete details. However, where we could, we've given you a rule of thumb—a brief guide that you can use quickly any time you need to compose a good piece of business writing.

PART
ONE

THE WRITING
PROCESS

1 WRITING IN THE BUSINESS WORLD

Most of the time, you must grab the attention of your reader immediately, or your carefully written material will end up in the recycling bin.

Writing in the business world is not like the writing that succeeds with teachers. In school, you write to demonstrate what you have learned. Teachers usually give you a chance to prove yourself. Remember the math teacher who gave you partial credit for a wrong answer if you had followed the correct procedure? You can't, however, assume that your audience in the business world will be so lenient. You need to put your best effort into every single document you write.

Know what you're talking about. Everything you write must be grounded in your sure knowledge of what is true. You can't fake it, so do your homework before you write.

Take care of errors in punctuation and word usage. Make everything you write as perfect as possible. Errors in spelling and grammar—even in e-mails and informal memos—will always work against you.

Follow the basic business forms and protocols. Creativity is often welcomed in projects, but each professional field follows standard presentation formats. Your office may have a "style sheet"—rules and formats your company has adopted—or there may be sample documents that you can use as guidelines.

Be positive. Most business writing attempts to solve a problem. You should try to be constructive, to praise others where praise is merited, and to offer criticism in terms that are helpful.

■ IDENTIFY THE KINDS OF WRITING YOU MUST DO

Whether you are new to the business world, or are a seasoned veteran, you can benefit from analyzing the kinds of writing required at your office. Examine the current files or seek out a senior colleague who does a lot of writing on the job and who is willing to serve as a mentor.

Categorize the types of documents you regularly must produce both by content and by the types of audience. Take a look at the Table of Contents of this book to see what chapters can best help you become a better writer.

■ KEEP YOUR READER IN MIND

In many cases, you know who will be reading your memo or report—a specific person or group—and can tailor your style and information accordingly. Knowing your reader allows you to

- Adopt an appropriate style—formal or friendly.
- Stress points your reader will care about.
- Explain points your reader may not know about.
- Address questions and concerns you expect this reader to raise.

Often, however, you do not know the specific person—for example, when writing a letter to a customer. Even when you do know the reader, someone else may see what you write—either now or in the future. For these reasons, it's best to

- Strike a balance between being too informal or too formal.
- Avoid being unnecessarily negative or accusatory of others.
- Make each separate point clear and concise.
- Give credit for the work of others.

Writing is a form of office politics. Be aware of what you put into writing and of who may see it.

■ STAY ON TOP OF THE PAPER FLOW

Time spent reading and keeping files organized can contribute to your success in writing. Minimize the amount of time you spend shuffling paper.

- Find a regular time in your schedule for uninterrupted reading.

- Store a second set of copies of documents essential to a project or to your career in a separate, safe place.

- Store files electronically whenever possible. If your e-mail program doesn't provide an easy way to store your mail in folders, cut and paste important messages into another program.

- Be smart about paper copies. Often, it is most efficient to print out a document and work on the hard copy, then enter the changes electronically. Some print documents should always be kept on file.

- Purge paper and electronic files regularly.

2   Finding Your Focus

Time spent before you start writing saves time and energy later.

Before you begin any writing project, take a few moments to assess the following characteristics.

■ The Importance of the Project

Who is the intended audience? A report intended for potential customers obviously warrants far more time and psychic energy than a summary of a meeting to be distributed to colleagues.

What is the expected life span of the document? An evaluation that will be part of an employee's personnel file requires more care than a thank-you note. You may want to save a well-written report to present as a justification for your promotion.

What is the purpose? Will you be writing to inform or to persuade? The latter requires more effort.

■ The Specific Requirements of the Project

Is creativity required? In some organizations, originality or style may be primary considerations.

Is collaboration required? If so, you will need to consider the schedules and personalities of the people involved. See Chapter 33, "Collaborative Projects."

How polished does it have to be? Keep your perspective. Don't allow a low-level but urgent project to take time from a more important one with a later deadline. Expend the right amount of energy necessary for the project to be successful, being careful to conserve enough of your energy for other important projects.

However, remember that your writing reflects on you; errors, even in an e-mail, indicate to some readers that you don't care enough—that you do not bother to get details right.

■ The General Requirements of the Project

Tone Your audience and purpose determine whether you will need to use a formal or informal tone, and whether you will need to spend great care on your phrasing.

Format Letters are usually more formal than memos; e-mail messages are even less formal—and often short lived. Reports can be a variety of types, sometimes requiring graphics or artwork.

Expected length Keep in mind that often a short piece of writing requires more effort than a long one. Readers prefer short documents; however, when given an assigned word- or page-count, you should conform. For tips on how to adjust length, see Chapter 9, "Revising."

■ The Deadline

Count back from the due date and assess how much time you have for gathering information, drafting, revising, and editing. The length of the product does not determine the production time. If, in spite of all your best efforts, you find yourself unable to meet the deadline, be sure to inform in writing everyone concerned.

3   SIZING UP YOUR WORK STYLE

To face any writing assignment effectively, you must first face yourself and own up to your actual work style.

The writing process requires four distinct phases:

- Developing your points and a plan
- Producing a first draft
- Revising—polishing for logic and style
- Editing—fine-tuning for correctness

Some writers move step-by-step through each phase of the project. They dislike chaos and prefer to work steadily, spreading the work over the full time available. Other writers, however, get excellent results by putting themselves under last-minute pressure. They thrive on tension and excitement. They often work out of order, moving back and forth, writing different parts and reorganizing as they go.

A particular *result* may look the same to an outsider, regardless of the method that produced it. What is important is to identify your own personal quirks and to make the most of your work style.

■ PROCRASTINATORS AND PERFECTIONISTS: WHAT TO DO ABOUT YOUR WORK STYLE

IF YOU ARE A PROCRASTINATOR

The advantages to procrastination are intensity, concentration, and a sense of adventure. The disadvantages are well known to all procrastinators and their families. A few shortcuts for the chronic procrastinator follow.

Accept that you don't have the luxury of time. Recognize that some aspects of a project may have to be correct but only "good enough," or that some people won't be able to collaborate according to your schedule.

Do at least one thing ahead of time. Pick one step that you don't mind too much and get it out of the way early. Decide on the format, do one freewrite, or read one background article. Pat yourself on the back for having accomplished one part of the job.

Keep a place for each project. As you work, put all the materials for the project in one designated space. Make copies of any documents that apply to more than one project, so that each project has a complete set.

IF YOU ARE A PERFECTIONIST

The great advantage of being thorough is that you have time to do a good job. The trick is to stay open, to let creativity bubble up, and to avoid filling time with unnecessary work. Here are some tips:

Don't let panic cloud your judgment. You can reduce a mountainous, overwhelming project to a series of manageable steps.

Don't organize or outline too soon. Allow the creative process to work for you by accepting a time of chaos while you gather ideas, talk to colleagues, do some research, and "sleep on it" a while. During this process, keep a notebook handy so that scraps of information and ideas don't get lost.

■ GUIDELINES FOR BOTH PROCRASTINATORS AND PERFECTIONISTS

Don't try to make only one draft. You may think you can save time by writing only one draft, but you can't get everything perfect the first time. Actually, it's faster to write something approximately close to the points you want to make, then go back and revise.

Don't get stuck trying to perfect your opening sentence or introductory paragraphs. You can always come back to the introduction once you see how the whole project turns out.

Don't use a dictionary, thesaurus, or grammarcheck before the second draft. Delay your concern for precise word usage and correct mechanics until you have the whole first draft written. Then, go back and make improvements.

Don't write with distractions. When you write, you need to focus your physical and mental energy. You can be distracted by background noise or by being too uncomfortable or too comfortable. You may not even realize how much these distractions can diffuse your energy and concentration.

Know when to quit. Be realistic about the approaching deadline and your own energy level. Allow some additional time for unexpected problems and for fine-tuning your manuscript.

Be smart about files and copies. Until the project is accepted, keep all notes and working documents. Afterward, don't file anything that someone else will keep for you in an easily accessed place. Many documents have already been stored in libraries or elsewhere—in electronic and paper formats, and in several secure locations. Finally, remember that e-mail that you have deleted is still in the company/service provider file.

4 What to Do When You're Stuck

For most writers, either *freewriting* (writing nonstop without a plan for ten to twenty minutes) or *brainstorming* (playing with lists of possibilities) will bring good ideas to the surface and show you the way to go.

Blocks in the flow of paper in an office aren't always just a matter of logjams due to volume. Very often, these blocks are not paper blocks, but writing blocks. Sometimes the ideas don't seem to be there, or you have only two ideas, or your thoughts are disconnected and jumbled. Sometimes it's hard to know where to begin or what shape your writing should take.

Here are some techniques used by professional writers. Try several— some are better for particular writing tasks. For instance, *lists* and *outlines* work when you don't have much time or when you have many points to include. Freewriting works well when your topic is subtle, when you want to write with depth. You'll find several techniques that work for you.

■ Divide the Project into Easy Steps

You can take an intimidating assignment one step at a time. Start wherever you're most comfortable. Often, once you have some ideas written, one will lead to another, and you'll soon have a whole draft to work with. Otherwise, try several of the following techniques.

■ Freewrite

Freewriting takes time, but it is the easiest way to begin and leads to surprising and creative results. In this method, you find your ideas by writing with no plan. Just write nonstop for ten to twenty minutes. Ignore grammar, spelling, and organization. Follow your thoughts as they come. Above all, don't stop! If you hit a blank place, write your last word over and over—you'll soon have a new idea.

After you have freewritten several times, read what you've written and mark the sentences that seem to contain your best thoughts.

Make a list of them and think further about each idea. Sometimes, a freewrite can contain the nucleus of a single important idea. Look for this unifying idea and write it at the top of your freewrite.

■ BRAINSTORM: MAKE LISTS, OUTLINES, OR MAPS

With this method, before you write any sentences, you make a list of your points, including any examples and details that come to mind. Jot them down briefly, a word or phrase for each item. Keeping these points brief makes them easier to read and rearrange. Include any ideas you think of—reject nothing for now. When you run dry, wait a little until more ideas come.

Now, start grouping the items on the list. Draw lines connecting examples to the points they illustrate. You may prefer to make a tree with branches and subtopics growing from the appropriate branch—or interlocking circles or other designs that "map" your ideas.

Then make a new list with the related points grouped together. Decide which idea is most important and cross out unrelated ideas or details. Arrange your points so that each will lead to the next. Be sure to note where examples or facts will be necessary to support your ideas.

You're ready to write. You'll see that this system works best when you have a big topic with many details. It also works best when you only have an hour to write a letter or a memo. Although it seems complicated, it actually saves time. Once you have your plan, the writing will go very fast.

If no coherent plan emerges, take a look at Chapters 2 and 5 ("Finding Your Focus" and "Organizing Your Ideas"). One of the approaches described there may be just right.

■ OTHER TECHNIQUES TO TRY

DO SOME RESEARCH

You may be stuck because you need more information. Pick up the phone or e-mail someone who can give you some facts. Spend an hour on the Internet or at your local or office library. Sometimes, just reading related information will give your ideas a jump start.

TALK TO A COLLEAGUE

The idea here is for your colleague to help you discover and organize your ideas—not to tell you his or her ideas. The best person for this technique is not necessarily someone who knows anything about the project, but someone who is a good listener. Ask the person just to listen and not say anything for a few minutes. As you talk, you might jot down points you make. Then ask what came across most vividly. Make notes of what you say in response. Once you have plenty of notes, you're ready to be alone and to freewrite or outline.

WRITE A SHORT DRAFT FIRST

In one page, write your ideas—everything you've considered including. Take just ten or twenty minutes. Now, you have a draft to work with. Expand each point with explanations or examples.

A simple technique is to write just one paragraph—at least six sentences—that tells the main ideas you have in mind. Arrange the sentences in a logical and effective sequence. Then, copy each sentence from that core paragraph onto its own page and write a paragraph or two to back up each sentence. Now, you have a rough draft. Remember, your first draft doesn't have to be perfect—as long as it's good enough for you to work with.

USE A TAPE RECORDER

If you have trouble writing as fast as you think, talk your ideas into a recorder. Play them back several times, stopping to write down the best sentences.

Another method is to write down four or five sentences before you begin, each starting with the main word of your topic, each different from the others. As you talk, use these sentences to get going when you run dry and to make sure you discuss different aspects of your topic.

5 ORGANIZING YOUR IDEAS

Your goal in organizing is to make sure that your reader gets your major points and that they are arranged in a logical sequence.

Readers in business often want only the point. In most cases, you must provide the rationale or the details, but those should be subordinated to a place where the busy reader can skim them. Headings, bulleted lists, and careful arrangement of your ideas will allow the reader to see the difference between the point and the supporting information.

■ HIGHLIGHTING YOUR MAIN POINTS

Before you do a final copy and send it to others, be certain that your main point or points stand out. They should be easily grasped even in a hasty reading.

- Before starting your final draft, write down the major point or points that you want your readers to get. Keep those points in front of you as you revise.

- Arrange a layout so that the main points are easily picked out by the eye. See Chapter 8, "Adding Visual Interest."

- Use a reference line (in memos, letters, and reports) to place your main point right up front and give it special emphasis.

- Repetition of a major point is often necessary in a long document. At times, you may choose to repeat a point to give it added weight. When you do repeat a point, make sure that you use slightly different wording and that you place each repetition in a different context.

■ CREATING A ROUGH OUTLINE

Some writers need an outline; others write first and then reorganize when they see a pattern in their writing. Still others begin in the middle or write the parts out of order. Some approaches are better for certain topics; some are better for certain audiences. You will need to discover the organization that best enhances the content.

Here's a method that works for many writers:

- Make a random list—written in phrases, not sentences—of all the ideas and facts you want to include. Don't be stingy. Make a long list.

- Decide which are your main points and which points support them.

- Cross off points from your list that do not fit. Remember, you can't put in everything you know without losing focus.

- Decide on your paragraphs—what each will demonstrate and their sequence.

- Now, start writing. Get a rough draft finished before you reconsider your organization.

■ WHEN TO ADJUST YOUR PLAN

Your main point may well shift and change as you write. Often, you will come up with better ideas, and as a result, you may change your emphasis. Be prepared to abandon parts or all of your original plan. Some minor points may now become major points.

Here are the signs that you should rethink the organization:

- Some parts are boring.

- Your real point doesn't show up until the end.

- You have repeated the same idea in several places—unless you have clearly done so for emphasis.

- The writing seems choppy and hard to follow.

- Your paragraphs are either too short or too long.

In the end, make sure that you know the main point you want the reader to get and that every sentence contributes to making that point clear.

▪ USING A FORMULA AS A PLAN

Ask yourself if you have done a similar project before. If so, you may be able to use the previous document as a model, or you may find other documents in the company files that you can use as a model. See Chapter 31, "Recurring Projects," for some techniques.

Some topics lend themselves to particular arrangements. Lengthy documents might even use different methods of organization in different sections.

COMMON PATTERNS OF ORGANIZATION

A list of points followed by detailed discussion (an introduction stating the main points, followed by a section on each point). This pattern is often used in a business proposal or in a letter of recommendation.

Good news/bad news This is a common method of organization, especially in the business world in which disappointing news so often must be communicated. The idea behind this pattern is that you begin with the positive and end with the negative. There may be times when you will want to reverse the order and end on a positive note.

Problem and solution You state the problem up front and then lay out the solution or solutions that you are recommending. At times, you may have to describe a number of less effective solutions to contrast with the solution you prefer.

Cause and effect As with problem/solution, you state the cause up front (or explain the "situation") and then enumerate the effects that will derive from this cause. (For example, explain a new company policy—the cause—followed by the specific effects this policy will have on employees.) You may reverse this pattern if your purpose is to explain the causes of something—a success or failure, for instance.

Chronology (the sequence in which events occurred). This is often the most logical order for laying out a problem, defending a decision, or persuading a reader to join a particular effort.

Narrative (the story that explains your main point). Telling the story is often used for performance evaluations, letters of recommendation, background, or informal newsletters.

Process (the specific steps for how something has been or should be done). Use this pattern whenever you give instructions or propose a project. Be certain that each step is logically and correctly arranged. See Chapter 24, "Instructions and Directions."

The news lead (the four Ws—*who, what, when, where*—always used in news articles). Sometimes *how* and *why* are included in the opening information. This is a good method to follow for most routine communications, such as announcements, memos, reports, minutes, and so on (who, what, when, where—followed by the details—plus how and why).

Comparison (similarities and differences). This pattern is especially useful when you have two distinct options for which you want to show the pros and cons. Comparison can also be used when you want to highlight or contrast the differences among several options.

Classification (types and categories). This is a useful organization when you have large amounts of information to communicate. Sometimes, information naturally falls into a particular classification; if not, you can always create logical categories as a way to organize material.

Generalization followed by examples or arguments Use this pattern when you want to build evidence in favor of your argument or example. You link your points to a main point; in other words, you move from the general to the specific. You can also reverse this pattern by beginning with specific arguments or examples and then ending with a general statement or idea that these specific examples suggest.

If what you want to say fits one of these patterns, following the pattern can help you organize more quickly.

6 PARAGRAPHING

Use paragraphs to lead the reader step-by-step through your ideas.

Each paragraph should make one point, and every sentence in it should relate to that one point. Usually the paragraph begins by stating the point and then goes on to explain it and make it specific.

Paragraphs should be as long as they need to be to make one point. Sometimes, one or two strong sentences can be enough. At other times, you might need as many as eight or more sentences to explain your point. Paragraphs give readers a visual landing, a place to pause; so use your eye and vary the lengths of your paragraphs. However, the trend in modern business writing is to avoid long paragraphs.

In business letters or reports, block format is the standard form:

- Single-space between the lines.
- Skip a line between the paragraphs.
- Do not indent the first line of paragraphs.

For example, this page uses block format.

■ FEATURE THE POINTS OF THE PARAGRAPH

When you have a number of points in a single paragraph, you can make them easy to follow.

ENUMERATE THEM

Your handling of this account has been extremely disappointing. First, Ms. Temple reports that you did not reply to e-mail or voice mail messages for days at a time. Second, when you did respond, you were abrupt and didn't allow her time to explain what she needed. Third, when the order you authorized finally arrived, it didn't meet the written specifications.

BREAK THEM OUT WITH BULLETS

> You have covered yourself with glory in handling Phil Blume's account:
>
> - The time you spent with him during the flood last month made rebuilding possible.
> - Your advice saved him time and money in the Johnson City plant.
> - Your professionalism and courtesy is the reason he is granting us the Amarillo project.

■ BREAK UP LONG PARAGRAPHS

A paragraph that is more than ten sentences usually should be divided. Find a natural point for division, such as:

- A subtopic

- A variation or contradiction

- The start of an example

■ EXPAND SHORT PARAGRAPHS

Too many short paragraphs can make your thought seem fragmented. If you have a string of paragraphs which consist of one or two sentences, you may need to combine, develop, or omit some of your paragraphs.

COMBINE

- Join two paragraphs about the same point.

- Include examples in the same paragraph as the point they illustrate.

- Regroup your major ideas and make a new paragraph plan.

DEVELOP

- Give examples or reasons to support your point.
- Cite facts, statistics, or evidence to support your point.
- Relate an incident or event that supports your point.
- Explain any important general terms.

OMIT

If you have a short paragraph that cannot be expanded or combined with another, chances are that paragraph should be dropped. Sometimes you have to decide whether you really want to explain a particular point or whether it's not important.

■ CHECK FOR CONTINUITY

Within a paragraph, make sure that your sentences follow a logical sequence. Each one should build on the previous one and lead to the next. Link your paragraphs together with transitions—taking words or ideas from one paragraph and using them at the beginning of the next one. See Chapter 7, "Continuity: Using Transitions," for help with transitions.

■ REMEMBER A BASIC PATTERN

If you have trouble with paragraph organization, you can usually rely on this basic paragraph pattern:

A main point stated in one sentence

An explanation of any general words in your main point

An example or details that support your point

The reason each example or detail supports your point

A sentence to sum up

Following is a sample paragraph illustrating this basic pattern.

We recommend that this traditional service station be replaced with a high-tech gas station/convenience store. By high-tech, we mean six pumps fitted with credit/ATM/cash machines, the latest pollution controls, and a secure monitor within the store. The volume on this corner will be better served by a facility geared toward sales, not repair service. A similar renovation of our Stewart Avenue station increased sales by 45 percent in the first six months of operation. The transformation could be completed by late spring 2000 if we follow the schedule that worked so well on Stewart Avenue.

7 CONTINUITY: USING TRANSITIONS

Transitions are bridges in your writing that take the reader from one thought to the next. These bridges link your ideas and provide continuity for your reader.

You need transitions between paragraphs that show the movement from one idea to the next, and you also need transitions to connect sentences within a paragraph.

Often, what seems like a continuity problem (the ideas feel choppy) is actually an organization problem. When your sequence of ideas and points is logical, transitions between the ideas come much more naturally and easily. Therefore, if one point doesn't fit smoothly, you may need to make a list of your points and toy with their order.

■ USE TRANSITION WORDS

Here are some choices of transition words you can use to illustrate certain points or relationships:

Adding a point:	furthermore, besides, finally, in addition to
Emphasis:	above all, indeed, in fact, in other words, most important
Time:	then, afterward, eventually, next, immediately, meanwhile, previously, already, often, since then, now, later, usually
Space:	next to, across, from, above, below, nearby, inside, beyond, between, surrounding
Cause and effect:	consequently, as a result, therefore, thus
Examples:	for example, for instance
Progression:	first, second, third, furthermore
Contrast:	but, however, in contrast, instead, nevertheless, on the other hand, though, still, unfortunately

Similarity:	like, also, likewise, similarly, as, then too
Concession:	although, yet, of course, after all, granted, while it is true
Conclusions:	therefore, to sum up, in brief, in general, in short, for these reasons, in retrospect, finally, in conclusion

■ Use Repetition of Key Words

- Repeat the word itself or variations of it.

   Everyone agrees that David Stevenson is intelligent. His intelligence, however, does not always endear him to his customers.

- Use pronouns.

   People who have hypoglycemia usually need to be on a special diet. They should, at the very least, avoid eating sugar.

- Use synonyms—different words with the same meaning.

   When you repot plants, be certain to use a high grade of potting soil. Plants need good rich dirt to thrive.

■ Use Transitional Sentences to Link Paragraphs

Usually the transition between paragraphs comes in the first sentence of the new paragraph.

   Even though Ms. Barbieri followed all of these useful suggestions, she still ran into an unforeseen problem.

   Because of these results, the researchers decided to try a second experiment.

Notice that, in these examples, the first half of the sentence refers to a previous paragraph; the second half points to the paragraph that is beginning.

8 ADDING VISUAL INTEREST: LAYOUT AND ILLUSTRATIONS

Every document can be made more readable with a good layout.

Computers have made creating your own format and graphics an enjoyable challenge. Add to that possibility all of the charts, graphs, drawings, diagrams, and photographs readily available from other sources and you could easily get into the habit of illustrating your point in nearly every document that you write.

Although everyone loves to look at visuals, don't make the mistake of just filling up space with cute or interesting pictures that have nothing to do directly with what you have written. If you just stick in something to create interest, you could well take your reader away from the point you are making.

■ GUIDELINES FOR LAYOUT

Even if you are not using visuals in your document, you can enhance anything you write by creating a layout that will make your document appealing and easy to read. Keep these simple rules of layout in mind:

- Use a consistent and uniform layout throughout.
- Use bulleted lists to break up the text.
- Use boldfacing for major ideas and summary sentences.
- Use subheadings whenever possible, especially in a long document.
- Use data boxes to set off important material.
- Plan ahead for attachments to the document, such as appendices, forms, and other supporting materials.

Notice that we have used both bulleted lists and boldfacing of major ideas in this chapter, as well as in others. It is fine to combine layout methods so long as you are consistent throughout the document. Be sure, however, not to overuse any of these features.

■ GUIDELINES FOR INCORPORATING VISUALS

Make sure each visual has a definite purpose. A visual should either give additional information or clarify information.

Keep it simple. Each visual should communicate a single idea. Also, beware of overusing a feature: bulleted lists and boldface can become monotonous.

Place visuals into the text right at the point they support—or place them all together in an appendix at the end. Place a commentary and explanation of each visual right above or below it. If you prefer to put all of the visuals in an appendix at the end, insert a reference for each visual into your text at the appropriate place.

Give the source of the illustration. Get permission before you publish copyrighted visuals. Beneath the visual, give information on where you found it: title of publication, author, publishing information, and page number. See Chapter 30, "Crediting Outside Sources," for proper documentation.

9 REVISING

Revision is not just fixing errors. It means taking a fresh look at all aspects of your writing, moving some parts of it, and completely rewriting others.

This chapter can serve as a checklist for any document you write, whether short or long. First read your draft aloud; then examine it from the following angles.

■ YOUR POINTS

- What is the most important point? Make sure it is prominently positioned and emphasized.

- Look for any points that are repeated or unrelated. Make appropriate cuts.

- Make sure your conclusion puts what you've written into perspective.

■ YOUR AUDIENCE

Even if this is a formal report for a faceless, mass audience, imagine a person actually reading your report.

- The opening line should snag the reader's interest.

- Look for places that sound stiff or artificial. Write the way you would talk to this person.

- Use *you* and *I* or *we*, if appropriate.

■ TROUBLE SPOTS

Look at the parts that are giving you trouble.

- Do you really need them? Are they in the right place?

- If you got tangled up trying to say something that you consider important, stop and ask yourself, "What is it I'm trying to say, after all?" Then, say it to yourself in plain English and write it down that way.

■ Length

HOW TO MAKE YOUR DOCUMENT SHORTER

Usually, business writing needs to be concise and easy to grasp—as a courtesy to the reader.

- Look for repetition. There is no need to give the same information in more than one place unless you are clearly doing so for emphasis.

- Remember your reader. How much does your specific reader need or want to know? Look for minor information that might bore your reader or distract from the main facts.

- Don't pad your writing. See Chapter 14, "Trimming Wordiness."

HOW TO MAKE YOUR DOCUMENT LONGER

Adding words and phrases to a report makes it, at most, an inch longer. Adding new points or new examples will make it grow half a page at a time.

- Build up what's good. Select the good parts, and write more about them.

- Add an example or explain your reasons to clarify your point—or even add a new point.

- Mention other views of the subject that differ from yours. Either incorporate them (showing the evidence for them) or disprove them (telling why others might accept them and why you reject them).

- Add details (facts, events that happened, things you can see or hear). Details are the life of good writing. Instead of writing, "Ms. Aznavour is a real team player," write, "Ms. Aznavour worked on the Collins account with four others. I observed how she filled in during a colleague's absence, met the holiday deadline in spite of a delay in shipping, and did all this with good humor."

- Expand your conclusion. Discuss implications and questions that your report brings to mind.

but

- Don't add empty phrases, because they make writing boring. Make sure that you're adding real content.

◼ CLARITY

- Look for places where your reader might not be able to follow your reasoning.

- Make sure you've demonstrated each point with specific details.

- If you expect a response, be sure you've spelled it out.

◼ STYLE

- Make sure that you've written with energy, using strong verbs, short snappy sentences, and brief paragraphs. See Chapter 13, "Writing with Energy."

- Use transitions (such as *accordingly, therefore, nevertheless*) to show the relationship between ideas. See Chapter 7, "Continuity."

- Write important sentences several ways until you find the best phrasing. See Chapter 17, "Varying Your Sentences."

◼ FORMAT

- How does the final product shape up? It should be easy on the eye.

- Use headings or bullets to emphasize key points.

- Your readers should be able to quickly find out what they want to know.

10 PROOFREADING

The key to proofreading is doing it several times.

Careless errors undermine what you have said, so make a practice of proofreading methodically.

Here are some tips to help you spot mistakes.

■ MAKE A BREAK BETWEEN WRITING AND PROOFREADING

Always put a little distance between the writing of a document and the proofreading of it. Set the project aside—at least for twenty minutes if you can. That way, you'll see it fresh and catch errors you otherwise might have overlooked. When you write under a deadline, train yourself not to write until the final moment; give yourself at least a few minutes to catch your breath. Then proofread your document several times before sending it.

■ USE YOUR COMPUTER'S CHECKING PROGRAMS

Although they aren't infallible, spellchecks and grammarchecks can help you locate obvious errors.

Be very conscious of how the automatic correction feature operates: The computer is often oblivious to context and may have changed your mistyped *for* to *of*. It will not alert you to a correctly spelled but inappropriate word—like *accept* versus *except* or *pour* versus *pore*. See Chapters 37 and 38, "Confusing Words" and "One Word or Two?"

■ SEARCH FOR TROUBLE

Assume that you have made unconscious errors and really look for them. Slow down your reading considerably, and actually look at every word.

■ Proofread for One Type of Error

If punctuation is your biggest problem, or if you always leave off *-ing* endings when you type, or if you always write *it's* for *its*, go through the document checking for just that one problem. Then go back and proofread to check for other mistakes.

■ Proofread out of Order

Try starting with the last sentence and reading backward to the first sentence; or proofread the second half first (usually, that's where most errors occur), take a break, and then proofread the first half.

■ Proofread Aloud

Always try to read your document aloud at least once. This will slow you down, and you'll hear the difference between what you meant to write and what you actually wrote.

■ Look Up Anything You're Not Sure Of

Use this book and a dictionary.

■ Proofread on Both Computer Screen and Page

First, scroll through and make corrections on the screen. Double-check places where you have inserted or deleted material. Because the eye is more accustomed to noticing errors on paper, you should print and proofread a draft copy of all important documents before sending them.

■ PROOFREAD YOUR FINAL HARD COPY SEVERAL TIMES

It does no good to proofread a draft of your document and then forget to proofread the final hard copy. This problem crops up often, especially under pressures of deadline. Remember: A typo is just as much an error as any other error.

PART
TWO

WRITING
WITH POWER

11 Steps Toward a Clear Style

Readers have little patience for having to search for a point. Be brief, direct, and concrete.

Clarity ought to be the number one goal in all business writing. Because most of the time you will be relating information, make sure that the information you give is absolutely clear.

■ Give Your Reader the Picture

Write for people—real ones. Think of your specific readers and "talk" to them on paper.

Don't delay or bury your point. Instead, be direct and straightforward. Start right off with what you have to say.

Show **the reader what you mean.** Highlight the big fact or create a memorable picture with words.

■ Use Explanations and Examples

You know what you mean because your experience lies behind your statement. Add an example or explanation to share that experience with your reader.

> Mr. Llewelleyn trains his sales associates thoroughly. For example, he rotates all areas of departmental responsibility, pairing a newcomer with a seasoned staff member.

> This quarter was marginally successful—by that, I mean that although profits were slightly below those of the last quarter, that loss was offset by the improved efficiency of the billing department.

Sometimes a hypothetical example can support your point.

> What if when you retire your pension is inadequate to cover a catastrophic illness?

■ Make the Point Easy to Find

- Keep your paragraphs short.

- Use headings and bullets.

- Write short snappy sentences.

- Use simple concrete words.

- Emphasize your main idea in several places throughout.

■ Above All, Be Specific

Details give life to your ideas. As you write, you naturally concentrate on your ideas, but the reader will best remember a strong example or fact. Therefore, underscore each major idea with strong details.

- A memorable fact

    The corporation's first business venture was not in real estate financing but in developing a biodegradable laundry detergent.

- A statistic

    Less than half a century ago, the company employed only 3 people; today, it employs 153,000.

- An anecdote

    Before Mavis Long and Peggy Schultz began their successful bridal consulting business, they were two housewives who had never worked outside their homes. Suddenly, they found themselves with lots of spare time and a major skill they'd developed over the years: planning weddings from start to finish.

- A real-life example

    Trang Lee arrived in this country with little English but incredible musical skills. The enclosed CD demonstrates how appropriate his style is for this project.

- A theoretical example

    Imagine a state-of-the-art, multimedia presentation that won't decimate your profits.

- An explanation of an abstract or technical term

   By vision, I mean that Carly has both a clear sense of each client's needs and an accurate view of the goals of each project.

This simple goal of being clear develops power in your writing.

12 Writing to Persuade

The art of persuasion stands at the core of nearly all business writing.

Most writing intends to either inform, entertain, or persuade. The best writing combines all three. Although you may think of business writing as primarily imparting information, a close look will usually reveal a subtle request or a streak of soft-sell persuasion.

Even a memo announcing an upcoming meeting will often contain the essential information and then a "push" for attending the meeting:

> This is the Benefits Committee's final meeting of the fiscal year, and we have several very important decisions to make. Please be there!

This is persuasion in its simplest form. Just being aware of some of the principles of persuasion can add power to everything you write.

■ Clarify the Outcome You Want

For everything you write, ask yourself what is at stake.

- Are you requesting information?

- Are you asking for specific action?

- Are you trying to change or influence another's opinion?

If you're trying to do any of the above, you will want to consciously use persuasion to bring about the desired outcome.

Ask yourself: What do I want to happen as a result of this communication? Write down the answer as clearly as possible and then keep it before you as you develop your communication. Keeping this single objective in mind will automatically sharpen your writing. For example, your objective may be as simple as one of these:

> I want the company to win this account without having to drop our prices.

I want the manufacturer to replace the copy machine with a new one and to give us a discount for all the frustration we've been put through.

I want upper management to provide a day care center within the building. It will eventually pay for itself in improved job attendance.

I want to be promoted to the new position. I meet all the qualifications and feel that I have earned this promotion because of my accomplishments for the corporation over the past three years.

■ TARGET YOUR AUDIENCE

Be certain you know who will be reading and reacting to your communication. In the business world, you rarely write for one person alone; usually, what you write will be circulated among managers, committees, departments, and so forth.

Remember that most businesspeople are extremely busy and impatient with long documents. Think about the people who will read your document. Are they already aware of your position and receptive to your arguments? Obviously, no group of people will have the same characteristics, but if you think of them as individuals and put yourself in their places, you will come up with a piece of writing that will be effective.

■ DEVELOP A STRATEGY

Sometimes you can persuade just by asking for what you want and then supplying the rationale, but often you will need to be more subtle. If you are dealing with a reluctant, even hostile audience, you'll need a thoughtful approach. It may be more effective to come at the subject softly or indirectly. For example, you might first want to explain the needs for a given course of action before presenting the recommended action.

However, if you are dealing with a highly charged situation, carefully rethink your strategy. Sometimes a face-to-face meeting might be the best first approach.

■ OPEN APPROPRIATELY

Gain your reader's attention and goodwill before launching into your arguments. Here are some possibilities.

- Open with a fact.

   The average business worker has 3,000 e-mail messages on file. (Selling a training session to raise employee consciousness about the legal issues related to e-mail messages)

- Begin with your most persuasive point.

   We all know that parking problems are a factor in employee tardiness. (For a proposed shuttle bus service)

- Begin with a story or metaphor.

   Fran Perry is a typical account executive. Her day begins. . . . (For an argument for an employees' day care center)

- Begin with a question.

   Could you use more reading time? (Proposing an audiotape library for the office gym)

- Open with a startling comment.

   I'll bet you didn't know that the average Canada goose defecates every three minutes. (A request for a new policy for the Municipal Parks Department)

- Begin directly with what you are seeking.

   I am writing this letter to ask you to vote against the proposed change of vendors. Here are the reasons why I am against this change:

■ STRIKE A POSITIVE TONE

In writing to persuade, it is particularly important that you use an inviting (that is, not alienating) tone of voice. It is possible to argue your point of view without offending others. You can be both polite and strong at the same time.

Use a conversational tone without being too informal or too ingratiating. Strive to sound like yourself—your very best self, your persuasive self. Ask for what you want in a direct, yet harmonious, way.

■ BUILD YOUR EVIDENCE

In building the evidence to support your request or point of view, you will make a stronger case if you follow these general guidelines:

- Make very clear what you are requesting your readers to do and give strong reasons why they should comply with your requests.

- Emphasize the benefits you expect (who will benefit and how).

- Don't confuse the issue by adding unnecessary details or arguments.

- Use facts and statistics to back up your position.

Give each point a separate paragraph. If you have more than two or three points—or arguments—you may want to consider using a heading above each paragraph so that your main points can be quickly read.

Decide on the order of your points. Sometimes, all the arguments are of equal value; if so, present them first in a bulleted list. Usually, however, there is one you will consider the most important. If so, put your major idea up front, just in case your readers only skim the document.

■ END WITH AN OPEN DOOR

You can never assume that you have persuaded your readers. Persuasion often takes place over time, and some communications will require follow-up letters, meetings, or phone calls. However, no matter how carefully you have presented your ideas, there will be times when you will fail to persuade others to your point of view.

Even when the news is "no," you will want to get that news as quickly as possible. Therefore, it's best to always end your persuasive document on a conciliatory note. Invite your readers to respond as honestly and as directly as possible, and make it clear that—whatever they decide at present—you are still open to future negotiations on the subject.

Note: If you are presenting your evidence in a lengthy document, add a short cover letter in which you clearly but briefly state your position.

13 WRITING WITH ENERGY

Good business writing is straightforward. Your readers will appreciate the truth, shared with simplicity by a writer who has given the topic attention and has decided what is important.

■ USE A CONVERSATIONAL TONE

Good writing has the feel of a real person talking—warm, natural, and direct. Excessive formality makes your writing stilted and difficult to read. However, this doesn't mean that you should use slang, sarcasm, or little jokes. Find a balanced approach that is appropriate for your audience.

A great technique for developing your own voice is to read your work aloud. If you do it regularly, you'll begin to notice when other voices are intruding or when you are using roundabout phrases. In time, your sentences will gain rhythm and force. Reading aloud helps you to remember that, when you write, you are, after all, telling something to somebody.

Keep these questions in mind:

- Am I saying this in plain English?

- Are these words that I normally use?

- Am I saying what I know to be true instead of avoiding the real issues?

■ BE DIRECT

Avoid confusion; say what you mean.

Use Personal Pronouns (*I, We, You*) Whenever You Can

Confusing: The main order of business was taken under discussion before a vote was taken on the four proposals.

> *Direct:*   We discussed the main order of business and then voted on the four proposals.

However, do not hide behind *we* when you really mean *I*.

Tell What Something Is, Rather Than What It Isn't

> *Confusing:*   The job description for deputy associate director does not meet the guidelines as discussed in the meeting.

> *Direct:*   The job description for deputy associate director must be rewritten to conform to the guidelines we discussed in the meeting.

> *Confusing:*   It is requested that this machine not be used for making personal copies.

> *Direct:*   This machine is for business use only.

Use Direct Questions

Replace implied questions with direct ones and your writing will sound more like a real conversation. An added bonus is that you will often get real information from your readers.

> *Indirect:*   We welcome your comments.

> *Direct:*   Do you have any comments? If so, please let us know.

> *Indirect:*   Please determine whether we are responsible for undelivered back orders.

> *Direct:*   Are we responsible for undelivered back orders? Please let us know.

■ CHOOSE ACTIVE VERBS WHENEVER POSSIBLE

You can write a verb in active or passive voice. Active is direct, passive more roundabout:

Passive: An inspiring talk was given at the luncheon.

Active: Greta Muse gave an inspiring talk at the luncheon.

Sometimes, the passive voice is necessary—when you do not know or are not at liberty to say who is doing the action.

Passive: A pedestrian was struck down at the intersection.

Passive: *Being* verbs are used to create the passive voice.

However, business writers sometimes use the passive voice because they think it sounds more "objective" and "official" sounding. It also sometimes has the advantage of hiding responsibility or softening harsh news.

Passive: Mr. Theron Smith's position has been terminated effective Monday, April 16th.

More often than not, you can put energy into your writing by converting passive verbs into active ones whenever possible.

Passive: A one-day writing skills workshop will be planned by the in-service committee.

Active: The in-service committee will plan a one-day writing skills workshop.

■ Get Rid of *Being* Verbs

Being verbs, like *is* and *are,* sap the energy from your writing. They dilute your sentences.

Look out for *am, is, are, was, were, be, being, been.*

Especially watch out for *there is, there are, there were, it is, it was.*

Often you can replace *being* verbs with forceful verbs. Sometimes you will have to rewrite or combine several sentences.

Passive: It is important that we examine the future implications of merging these departments.

Active: We must examine the future implications of merging these departments.

Passive: The presentation was well received. The client was particularly impressed by the design of the logo.

Active: The client loved the presentation—particularly the design of the logo.

Whenever you can, replace limp verbs with dynamic verbs. The changes will energize your sentences.

14 TRIMMING WORDINESS

Often we think that people are impressed by a writer who uses big words and long sentences. Actually, people are more impressed by a writer who is *clear.*

Make it a habit to practice economy in your writing. Say exactly what you mean in as few words as possible without sacrificing necessary information.

■ MINIMIZE JARGON: REPLACE FANCY OR TECHNICAL WORDS

Within a specialized field, technical terminology has its rightful place. It can save time and effort because it is instantly recognizable by the people within that field. However, even when you are addressing fellow specialists, jargon can easily become confusing as well as boring; so strive to use everyday words as often as possible.

For example, replace

utilize with *use*   *necessitate* with *need*

conceptualize with *conceive*   *altercation* with *disagreement*

concur with *agree*   *interface* with *connect*

Jargon: With the reception of the new equipment, we will be enabled to conceptualize at least fifteen scaled drawings per day and thus gain a competitive edge against our competitors.

Clear: When we receive the new equipment, we will be able to produce at least fifteen scaled drawings per day and outperform our competitors.

When you do use a technical term for a general audience, be sure to define or explain it.

As land becomes more scarce, the field of hydroponics—the science of growing plants in liquid—will create many new career opportunities.

■ DELETE *THAT* AND *WHICH* WHEREVER YOU CAN

Elmo is the monster that most four-year-olds prefer.
Elmo is the monster most four-year-olds prefer.

The budget which I am submitting will clarify my philosophy.
I am submitting a budget to clarify my philosophy.

■ OMIT WORDS THAT SOUND GOOD BUT CARRY NO CLEAR MEANING

really	thing/something	proceeded to
absolutely	the fact that	shows a tendency to
wonderful	bring to a conclusion	is a person who
experience	at this point in time	in today's society
personality	with the result that	come to terms with
situation	expresses an opinion that	

Wordy: The reason Ms. Pawatti resigned was due to the fact that she was sick.

Trim: Ms. Pawatti resigned because of illness.

Wordy: In today's society, uncertainty is something we all fear.

Trim: We all fear uncertainty.

■ AVOID REDUNDANCY—POINTLESS REPETITION

Wordy: She gave birth to her baby at three A.M.

Trim: She gave birth at three A.M.

Wordy: The work counters are creamy beige in color and coordinate with the appliances.

Trim: The beige work counters coordinate with the appliances.

Wordy: Ms. Moffet does not seem able to have the personal authority required for this position.

Trim: Ms. Moffet lacks the personal authority for this position.

When you trim, don't worry that your writing will be too short. If you need length, add examples and further thoughts. Look at the topic from a different viewpoint. Add points, not just words.

15 GRAMMAR REVIEW: COMMON SENTENCE PATTERNS

Although simple sentences are often the most effective, good writing uses a variety of sentence patterns. Combine sentences to vary the rhythm or to show the interrelationship of several ideas.

■ SIMPLE SENTENCES

Each simple sentence contains a subject and a verb, which form the kernel of the sentence. Usually, a completer (a complement, direct object, or modifier) is added.

To control grammar, punctuation, and style, first identify the verb and then its subject. At the heart of every sentence—no matter how complicated—is a subject and a verb.

> We will move.
>
> Money talks.
>
> The delivery is late.

We, money, and *delivery* are the subjects; *will move, talks,* and *is* are the verbs. Notice that the verb enables the subject to do or be something. Strong writing features the verb—usually early in the sentence.

- In a command or a direction, the subject is understood to be "you"—the reader.

> Avoid submerging this product in water.
>
> Walk two blocks past the traffic light.

- Sentences can have more than one subject and more than one verb:

> Both our accountant and our marketing manager will attend the conference.
> (two subjects–*accountant* and *manager*)
>
> The designers will analyze your reception area and offer three new options.
> (two verbs–*analyze* and *offer*)

- Usually a word or phrase completes the subject and verb:

  Taneeka Moore supervises fifty-three auditors.

  It's not very difficult.

  This report says absolutely nothing.

  Regina swims every morning.

- Sometimes a word or group of words introduces the main part of a sentence:

  However, the entertainment expenses have been disallowed.

  For example, we use only organic produce.

  In the packet labeled "Open First," you'll find the necessary tools.

■ COMPOUND SENTENCES

You can join two related sentences with a comma plus a coordinating conjunction, or with a semicolon. The result gives equal weight to the point each sentence makes.

COMMA PLUS COORDINATING CONJUNCTION

A coordinating conjunction establishes a specific relationship between two sentences.

> *Sentence, [coordinating conjunction] sentence.*

Coordinating Conjunctions

and but or nor for so yet

> I prefer the French wallpaper, but Margaret doesn't care for it.
>
> I prefer the French wallpaper, so that's what I'm ordering.
>
> I prefer the French wallpaper, yet I'm open to other patterns.

Note that without the coordinating conjunction, the comma is inadequate; a semicolon is then required.

SEMICOLON

A semicolon can be used instead of a period between two closely related sentences.

> *Sentence; sentence.*

> I prefer the French wallpaper; it is within our budget.

> The committee recommends Bruce Urquhart; our explanation is attached.

Often, a transition word—a conjunctive adverb—is used to provide smoothness following a semicolon. A comma before these words is not sufficient to join two sentences.

Conjunctive Adverbs

however   therefore   thus   nevertheless   indeed   then   besides

> I prefer the French wallpaper; besides, it is within our budget.

> I prefer the French wallpaper; however, Margaret doesn't care for it.

Conjunctive adverbs are often used within sentences rather than between them.

> Margaret, however, doesn't care for the French wallpaper.

> The decision, therefore, is irrevocable.

> The Internet, nevertheless, is the primary vending market for this product.

■ COMPLEX OR SUBORDINATE SENTENCES

Two sentences can be joined if one is preceded by a subordinating word.

> *[Subordinating Word] sentence, sentence.*

> *Sentence [subordinating word] sentence.*

Subordinating Words

because   although   if   whereas   when   before   after   while

A complex sentence has two parts:

- A main sentence—a complete sentence that can stand alone

- A subordinated sentence—a sentence introduced by a subordinating word and which, therefore, cannot stand alone

> The primary market for sea urchins is Japan although they are harvested in Maine.

Notice that the parts are reversible.

> Although they are harvested in Maine, the primary market for sea urchins is Japan.

Note that when the subordinating word is in the middle, no comma is necessary.

> When the annual reports arrive from the printer, they must be stored temporarily in the conference room.

> The annual reports must be stored temporarily in the conference room when they arrive from the printer.

> After the morning conference ends, we'd be pleased to have you as guests for lunch.

> We'd be pleased to have you as guests for lunch after the morning conference ends.

■ COMPOUND–COMPLEX SENTENCES

A compound-complex sentence occurs when one or both halves of a compound sentence have subordinated parts.

> Although we had heard some unpleasant rumors, we planned to sign the contract; but we canceled when the truth came out.

> The piano has to be moved onto the stage a day ahead of time so it can be tuned twenty-four hours before the concert begins.

■ USING *BUT, HOWEVER, ALTHOUGH*

But is a coordinating conjunction; *however* is a conjunctive adverb; *although* is a subordinating conjunction.

> These three words are used to reverse the meaning of a sentence, but they are punctuated differently.

> These three words are used to reverse the meaning of a sentence; however, they are punctuated differently.

> These three words are used to reverse the meaning of a sentence although they are punctuated differently.

For an illustration of sentence structure, see "Anatomy of a Sentence" in the appendix of this book.

16 AVOIDING TANGLED SENTENCES

Look at your sentences to make sure that the parts go together.

■ ERRORS IN PARALLEL STRUCTURE

Strong sentences often use a list or a pair; the parts must be in the same format. Sentences with parallel structure repeat the same word or grammatical structure within a single sentence.

> Coming to terms with a problem is not always the same as coming to terms with its solution.

> Thalia recommends that we increase the budgets for print advertising, for new logo designs, and for calling former customers.

> *Not parallel:* Ms. Bronson could always be relied upon to meet her deadlines, to develop creative solutions, and always provided a fresh perspective on relationships with our clients.

Here, two verbs have *to,* but the last has no *to* but instead, an *-ed* ending. The first and last phrases have *always,* but the middle one doesn't.

> *Parallel:* Ms. Bronson could always be relied upon to meet her deadlines, to develop creative solutions, and to provide a fresh perspective on relationships with our clients.

> *Not parallel:* First, assemble all ingredients: butter, sugar, baking powder, and eggs, and don't forget to sift the flour.

Here, all the parts of the list should be nouns.

> *Parallel:* First, assemble all ingredients: butter, sugar, baking powder, eggs, and sifted flour.

Parallel structure is especially important when composing headings, a bulleted list, or items in a résumé. For example, the headings in this chapter are all nouns or noun phrases; in Chapter 10, "Proofreading," the headings are all directions (imperative verbs begin all of them); in Chapter 6, "Paragraphing," the first two sets of bullets are sentences and the third set all nouns. The point is that within any group you must be consistent.

■ DANGLERS

There are two problems. In one, a word (often a pronoun) has been left out, so that the introductory phrase doesn't fit with what follows.

> *Dangler:* Having won three design awards, the commission to do the renovation of the post office was an additional accolade.

This sounds as if the commission won the awards. To correct it, add the missing word or words.

> *Correct:* Having won three design awards, the architects considered the commission to do the renovation of the post office an additional accolade.

> *Correct:* The architects had already won three design awards; the commission to do the renovation of the post office was an additional accolade.

The second problem occurs when a phrase or word in a sentence is too far from the part it goes with.

> *Dangler:* A former Congressional aide, our company found Brenda Watters to be a skillful leader.

This sounds as if the company is a former Congressional aide.

> *Correct:* A former Congressional aide, Brenda Watters has proved to be a skillful leader in our company.

■ Mixed Sentence Patterns

Sometimes you start with one way of getting to a point, but one of the words slides you into a different way of saying it. The two patterns get mixed up. Correct a mixed sentence pattern by using one pattern or the other.

Mixed
(Incorrect):   By using our innovative program allows smooth integration of e-mail and office files.

Here the writer started to say "By using our innovative program, you can integrate e-mail and office files," but the phrase *innovative program* took over.

Correct: Using our innovative program allows smooth integration of e-mail and office files.

Mixed
(Incorrect):   In the Republic of Cameroon has over 200 local languages.

Correct: The Republic of Cameroon has over 200 local languages.

Correct: In the Republic of Cameroon, over 200 local languages are spoken.

Note that, most often, these problem sentences begin with *by* or *in*.

17 VARYING YOUR SENTENCES

The same idea can be expressed in many different ways, and every sentence has movable parts.

To improve your style, try reading your writing aloud. When you come across choppy or monotonous sentences, use some of the following techniques.

■ WRITE AN IMPORTANT SENTENCE SEVERAL WAYS

You can turn a sentence that troubles you into a sentence that pleases you. Instead of fiddling with a word here and a word there, try writing five completely different sentences—each with the same idea. One could be long, one short, one a generalization, one a picture, and so forth. Often, you'll find that your first isn't your best. If you play with several possibilities, you'll come up with the one you want. This technique works especially well for improving introductions and conclusions.

■ USE SHORT SENTENCES FREQUENTLY

Short sentences are the meat and bones of good writing. Intersperse short sentences throughout your writing for clarity and strength.

- They can simplify an idea.

    All in all, the plan failed.

- They can dramatize a point.

    No one in the room uttered a protest.

- They can add rhythm.

    Everything went haywire. The lights blew out. Water spewed down from the sprinkler system.

- They can be blunt and forceful.

Another salary review is definitely in order.

If you're getting tangled in too many words, a few short sentences will often get you through.

■ Lengthen Choppy Sentences

Using only short sentences, nevertheless, can make your writing monotonous. If you want to lengthen a sentence, the simplest way is to add concrete information.

> Gina Popovic is our strongest editor.

> By signing prolific and popular authors, Gina Popovic has built the Female Private-Eye series into our strongest book list.

■ Combine Choppy Sentences

Combine two short sentences back-to-back. Here are three ways:

- Put a semicolon between them. (Be sure each half is a complete sentence.)

    > We are considering the use of heat pumps for this project; an alternative might be solar panels.

- Put a comma followed by one of these connectors:

but	and	so	yet
for	nor	or	

    > We are considering the use of heat pumps for this project, but an alternative might be solar panels.

- Put a semicolon followed by a transition word and a comma. Here are the most common transition words.

however	for example	meanwhile
therefore	furthermore	nevertheless
instead	in other words	on the other hand
besides		

    > We are considering the use of heat pumps for this project; however, an alternative might be solar panels.

■ COMBINE SENTENCES TO HIGHLIGHT THE MAJOR POINT

Often, sentences contain two or more facts. You can show the relationship between these facts so that the most important one stands out.

In these examples, two ideas are given equal weight.

> I recommend that we reconsider the February deadline. The ice storm has delayed everyone here.

> The small yellow tomatoes are difficult to obtain. Joe Dunn promises to deliver a bushel each week.

Here are the same ideas with one point emphasized.

> I recommend that we reconsider the February deadline because the ice storm has delayed everyone here.

> Even though small yellow tomatoes are difficult to obtain, Joe Dunn promises to deliver a bushel each week.

Notice that the halves of these sentences can be reversed.

> Because the ice storm has delayed everyone here, I recommend that we reconsider the February deadline.

> Joe Dunn promises to deliver a bushel of small yellow tomatoes each week—even though they are difficult to obtain.

Usually the sentence gains strength when the most interesting point comes last.

■ INSERT THE GIST OF ONE SENTENCE INSIDE ANOTHER

The problem with most choppy sentences is that one after another starts with the subject of the sentence. Sometimes you can use *who* (for people), *that* or *which* (for things) to start an insertion. Sometimes you can reduce the insertion to a word or phrase.

> The PS/2 port is at the back of the laptop. It can be used to connect an external mouse or keyboard.

> The PS/2 port, which is at the back of the laptop, can be used to connect an external mouse or keyboard.

> The PS/2 port, at the back of the laptop, can be used to connect an external mouse or keyboard.

To stress the most important parts of your sentence, tuck in interrupters or insertions. Put transitions or minor information into the middle of your sentence.

> He procrastinates, as we all have observed, yet always meets his deadline.

> From my point of view, however, that's a mistake.

> The concrete, for example, was of poor quality.

Remember to put commas on both sides of the insertion.

■ USE PARALLEL STRUCTURE

Parallel structure—repeating certain words for clarity and emphasis—makes elegant sentences.

> To be honest is not necessarily to be brutal.

In a list of parallel items, save the most important one for last.

> We are prepared to offer you continuation of your health insurance for two years, the use of your office and secretary for two months, and 250 percent of this year's salary.

Famous quotations are often based on parallel structure.

> I came, I saw, I conquered.
>
> —Julius Caesar

> To believe your own thought, to believe that what is true for you in your private heart is true for all men—that is genius.
>
> —Ralph Waldo Emerson

> Ask not what your country can do for you; ask what you can do for your country.
>
> —John F. Kennedy

For the correct usage of parallel structure, see Chapter 16, "Avoiding Tangled Sentences."

■ IMITATE GOOD WRITERS

Take a close look at the writings of some of your favorite authors. A good exercise is to pick out a sentence or a paragraph that you particularly like. Read it aloud once or twice; then, copy it over several times to get the feel of the language. Now, study it closely and try to write an imitation of it. Use the sentence or paragraph as a model, but think up your own ideas and words. This exercise can rapidly expand your power to vary your sentences.

18 Eliminating Biased Language

Biased language includes all expressions that demean or exclude people. To avoid offending your reader, examine both the words you use and their underlying assumptions.

■ Offensive Word Choices

Some wording is prejudiced, impolite, or outdated.

Eliminate name-calling, slurs, or derogatory nicknames. Instead, refer to groups by the names they use for themselves. For example, use women (not girls), African Americans (not colored people), Asians (not Orientals).

Replace words using *man* or the *-ess* ending with nonsexist terms. For example, use flight attendant (not stewardess), mechanic (not repairman), leader or diplomat (not statesman), humanity (not mankind).

■ False Assumptions

Some statements are based on hidden biases. Look hard at references to any group—even one you belong to. Check for stereotyping about innate abilities or flaws in members of a group. After all, every member of the group does not believe, look, or behave exactly like every other member. For example, all women are not maternal, all lawyers are not devious, all Southerners are not racist, and all Japanese are not industrious. Many clichés are based in stereotypes: absent-minded professor, dumb jock, Latin temper.

Check assumptions that certain jobs are best filled by certain ethnic groups or one sex. For example, all nurses aren't women; all mechanics aren't men; all ballet dancers aren't Russian.

Watch for inconsistency.

- In a pair:

    man and wife

Instead, use

> man and woman   or   husband and wife

- In a list:

> two Republicans, a Democrat, an Independent, a woman, and
> an African American

This list assumes that everyone is a white man unless otherwise specified. Instead, use

> three Republicans, two Democrats, and an Independent

■ Faulty Pronoun Usage

Check pronouns for bias.

> Each judge should have his clerk attend the conference.

- One option for revision is to use *his* or *her.*

> Each judge should have his or her clerk attend the conference.

- A better solution is to use the plural throughout.

> The judges should have their clerks attend the conference.

- Often, the most graceful solution is to eliminate the pronoun.

> Each judge should have a clerk attend the conference.

You can find more help with pronoun choice in Chapter 43, "Consistent Pronouns."

PART

THREE

SPECIFIC BUSINESS WRITING

19 Guidelines for All Business Correspondence

Here are a few basic rules for writing and managing all business correspondence.

Every single communication should feature the following:

- Current date (month, day, and year)

- Your full name and title

- Name of your business (and department or division)

- Your complete mailing address

- Telephone, e-mail, and fax numbers—including area codes (plus country codes for international correspondence)

- Person to contact if different from you

Present all the important information up front. When referring to a previous communication, recap the highlights.

> During our teleconference 11/6/98, you agreed to . . .
>
> In your memo of 2/14/99, you said . . .
>
> Re: Acct. 906-778-499 (Rock Design Inc.–Installation April-May 2000) . . .

When scheduling a meeting, include the following:

- Who should attend

- The location

- The day(s) of the week

- The complete date(s)

- The beginning and ending times with A.M. or P.M. plus, if necessary, the time zone

Take care of incoming correspondence.

Distinguish between the following:

- Documents that need a response

- Documents of temporary importance—for instance, information that you'll need to keep handy for a specific project

- Documents of lasting importance

Make hard copies of electronic documents important to your company or to your career, and consider storing copies in two locations for safety.

Discard duplicates of minor documents and, of course, discard anything that requires only one reading—or none.

20 E-MAIL AND FAX MESSAGES

Be very careful to distinguish between the more formal messages that may be retained on file and the casual ones sent between colleagues.

Before you click "send," be aware that innocuous little messages (as the writers initially considered them) can later turn up in lawsuits.

COMPLETE IDENTIFICATION

Every fax and e-mail should make it easy to reply in other ways. If your e-mail program doesn't have it, make a form that you can copy to the bottom of every business message you send. Use a similar form or your letterhead for faxes. Include the following:

- Your full name and title

- The company name and mailing address

- The phone, fax, and e-mail numbers

- The name and number of the person to contact regarding this message if different from you

THE SUBJECT LINE

The subject line for a fax should give enough information that the recipient won't have to consult all your previous correspondence in order to respond.

The subject line for e-mail needs to be short because many programs only show a few words as the new mail arrives. However, it still needs to be accurately phrased. There's nothing worse than learning that your urgent message was saved for evening reading because the recipient didn't know it was important.

Revise the automatic repetition of the original e-mail subject line if necessary to be clear when you reply to someone's message. Come up with a pithy line that suits your current message. Abbreviate if you have to.

Urgent–from Kenneth

Re: Mont. Fishing article

Change in NYer deadline

KEEPING THE MESSAGE BRIEF

- Give essential information up front.

- Use bullets and headings to make points easy to grasp.

- Trim unnecessary explanations and details.

- As you compose, keep in mind that your message may be retained or forwarded to others.

SALUTATION AND COMPLIMENTARY CLOSE

Use the format for letters or memos for fax messages; however, the etiquette for e-mail is still evolving. Here are your choices:

- You may omit both the greeting and the closure—as memos do— but most people don't, because it feels abrupt.

- You may begin and end as with a letter. For business communication—especially with strangers—it is preferable to retain the formalities.

  Dear Ms. Fayla:

  Truly yours, Tina Stone

- You may use a casual tone—appropriate with colleagues and established business acquaintances.

  Dorothy–

  Good Morning, Nathan!

  Best, James

  Talk to you Thursday. Samantha

PROOFREAD, PROOFREAD, PROOFREAD!

Compose an important message offline in your word-processing program where you can make corrections easily; then, paste it into your e-mail.

In any case, read the message carefully—at least twice.

ATTACHMENTS, JOKES, GRAPHICS

Send attachments, jokes, and memory-hogging graphics only if you're sure the person wants them.

COPIES

Copy the message only to those who need to know. Be aware that most people resent having to go through excessive messages, and some also do not want their e-mail addresses sent wholesale to those out of their preferred communication loop. Don't put colleagues on the spot by copying higher-ups unless you mean to do so.

BLIND COPIES

With blind copies, those recipients and their addresses are not listed on the other recipients' copies, allowing for privacy. You can also send a blind copy to yourself—handy when you are sending the message from a different computer and want to retain a copy of the message.

RICH TEXT FORMAT FOR ATTACHMENTS

Unless you are sure that the recipient shares your word-processing and other programs, send attachments in rich text format (RTF), which will retain most of the formatting.

MAINTAINING YOUR FILES

If your e-mail program doesn't allow you to organize your messages into folders, copy and paste important messages into your word-processing program where you can organize them.

Work out a system for deleting or keeping important messages. As they arrive, print out messages you need to keep on file or use to draft a response.

21 MEMOS

Memos are best for routine communications with colleagues—either in-house or to outsiders with whom you've established a business relationship.

Memos can range in tone from the very formal to the casual, but they are always more impersonal than a letter. Whenever you need to communicate any kind of sensitive or confidential information, always use a letter instead of a memo.

■ FOLLOW THE STANDARD FORM

HEADING

If you are not using a standard company memo form, devise a form that you can use and keep it stored in your computer. It should include the following, in this order:

- The full name of the company—and the address, for memos going outside the company

- The name of your department, if applicable

- The phrase "Interdepartmental Memorandum" (for memos outside your department) or "Intradepartmental Memorandum" (for memos within your department)—if appropriate

- The line indicators in boldface (which are then filled in for each new memo)

  Date:

  To:

  From:

  Subject:

BASIC ELEMENTS

Date Give the complete date, including the year. Abbreviations or all digits are acceptable.

12/3/99   12.3.99   Dec. 3, 1999   3 Dec. 1999

To List only those who are directly affected by the memo (as opposed to those you just need to inform). Give full names; give titles only if necessary for informing recipients who may not know some of the others.

From Give your full name; title; phone, fax, and e-mail numbers. Initial the final copy, in ink, right next to your name.

Subject Give as complete a description as possible, briefly worded.

> Subject: Breakfast meeting for all associates 7:45 A.M., Monday, 12/6/99 in T545—Honoring Annual Performance

or

> Re: Arizona filming delayed two weeks, revised schedule below

Body Keep paragraphs short. If you have written your subject line accurately, the rest of the memo need be only briefly informative or persuasive. If your message is complicated, use bullets or headings to break out key points. Attach agendas or schedules if necessary.

> The Desert 667 shoot scheduled for 10/2/99 has been rescheduled for 10/16/99.
>
> Model injured.
>
> Ms. Navidovovitch twisted her ankle. Her physician expects her to be fully recovered by our new deadline.
>
> Donkey wrangler is reneging on the contract.
>
> We have found a substitute burro—contract has been signed. Legal department has been given all details on the donkey.
>
> All other personnel and arrangements are in place.
>
> I assure you that all crews and equipment are ready for 6:00 A.M. MDT, 10/16/99—according to the newly updated contracts.
>
> Confirming paperwork is en route via separate correspondence.

Closure Do not use a complimentary close—as with a letter. You may use a brief closing remark as a conclusion.

Thank you for your attention to this matter.

Thursday's meeting will enable us to resolve the final details for the Harvest Festivities.

I will be in touch with everyone by Monday morning.

Signature Sign or initial beside your name on the *From* line. Do not add a signature line at the end of the memo (appropriate only for a memorandum of agreement or a formal letter).

Copy list (optional). List the names and titles of persons who will be sent copies of the memo. If they are not at your address, give their addresses as well. Keep this list as short as possible—on a need-to-know basis.

cc: Patsy Turner, Legal Dept.
Sarah Miles, Accounting Dept.
Spencer Hart, Jennifer Greene, Advertising Dept.

When you send the copies, highlight or check the name of the appropriate recipient.

Enclosure reminder (optional). If you have included additional documents, use the simple abbreviation *encl.* and an itemized list if there are several.

encl.: revised production schedule
revised contracts–to Legal Dept. only

▪ Memorandum of Agreement

A document in the memo format may serve as a contract, binding on both parties once they have signed below the description of their agreement. In this case, the memo is addressed to the business affiliations of the signatories and is sent from the individuals who signed. Here you do use signature lines and date of signing. Do not initial the *From* line.

22 LETTERS

Take time to compose a few basic letters that reflect your own personal approach and that sound like you.

Most business writers send out a few standard letters—over and over. There are templates (providing design and layout) in most word-processing programs—and even letters to copy. Unfortunately, the rest of the business world has access to those same standard letters. If you develop your own templates, including key sentences, all you'll have to do is change a few details for a personalized letter.

■ FOLLOW THE STANDARD FORM

HEADING

If you are not using company stationery with a letterhead, make a heading that you can copy to the top of each letter. It should include the following, attractively arranged (usually centered or aligned to the left, but it is also acceptable to arrange across the top of the page), in this order:

- Full name of the company

- Street address with suite or room number if appropriate

- City, state, and zip code (plus country for foreign correspondence)

- Phone, fax, and e-mail numbers

TYPEFACE

- Ordinarily, use No. 12 typeface on the computer.

- Do not use all capital letters or all italics.

SPACING

- Use an inch to an inch-and-a-half margin on all four sides.

- Single-space.

- Indicate the beginning of each paragraph by skipping a line and starting at the left margin (block format).

- Justify (line up the margin) only on the left. Justifying on the right distorts the spacing between letters and words, making the letter harder to read.

BASIC ELEMENTS

Date Give the full date without abbreviations.

September 28, 1999   **or**   28 September 1999

Addressee Give the person's full name and title, followed by the complete address. If you do not have a person's name, be as accurate about the title as possible.

Mr. Kevin Kim
Vice President of Marketing
Stylish Resortware, Inc.
1223 Avenue of the Americas
New York, NY 10021

Subject line (optional). Give a brief reference if it will simplify the opening sentence.

Re: Account ZH 48972-89

or

Re: Ms. Liza Greene's Promotion

Salutation Unless you are on a first-name basis, use the person's last name and title, followed by a colon. If you do not have the name, use the title.

Dear Mr. Kim:

or

Dear Vice President of Marketing:

Body Usually a letter contains two or more paragraphs. Keep paragraphs short for quick reading.

Second and subsequent pages The top right corner of each page after the first should contain an abbreviated title for the letter plus the page number.

L. Greene's Promotion, p. 2

Complimentary close Use one of the tried-and-true phrases.

> Very truly yours,
> Sincerely,
> Best wishes,
> Regards,

Signature space Your signature is necessary to authenticate the letter. Skip three to four lines after the complimentary close. Here you will write, by hand in ink, your usual signature—full name but without titles—unless you are on a first-name basis with the addressee. Do not underscore the signature line.

Typed line(s) with your full name and title

> Joanna Blossom
> Director of Human Resources

Copy list (optional). Skip a line and then list the names and titles of persons who will be sent copies of the correspondence. If they are not at your address, give their addresses as well.

> cc: Ms. Veronica Brooks
> Vice President of Human Resources
>
> Mr. Sam Chapin
> Equal Opportunity Office
> 1254 Dupont Circle
> Washington, DC 20015

When you send the copies, highlight or check the name of the recipient.

Typist's initials If you're typing a letter for someone else, give that person's initials in capitals followed by a colon and then your own initials in lower case.

> JL:efh

Enclosure reminder (optional). If you have included additional documents, use the simple abbreviation *encl.* and add an itemized list if there are several.

> encl.:   photocopy of resignation letter
> photocopy of original application
> photocopies of employment reviews, 1996, 1997

■ MAKE YOUR LETTER EASY TO READ

BEGIN WITH THE PURPOSE OF YOUR LETTER

> I am writing to report about the employment history of Ms. Carrie Young.

> Thank you for a very informative tour of your facilities.

> This letter is a formal request for a change in the packaging you use for our mushrooms.

BE CLEAR AND DIRECT

If you expect a particular outcome as a response to your letter, say so—politely, but up front. Use *I* and *you.*

> I expect your company to replace the entire 6/7/00 shipment, which was damaged because of your driver's negligence.

BE BRIEF

Give only those details necessary to explain your points.

END ON A PLEASANT NOTE

> I hope that we can come to a mutually beneficial agreement.

> Yours is the most impressive portfolio we have ever seen. Congratulations!

> Thank you for your personal attention to this matter.

■ USE INFORMAL HANDWRITTEN NOTES WHEN APPROPRIATE

Many occasions in business require a more personal response—even with someone you know only in a business context. Use these guidelines when thanking someone for an entertainment or when expressing a personal wish (such as congratulations, sympathy, holiday greetings):

The note should be handwritten in ink. It can be brief, and may be added to a short printed message on a card. It should be in your own handwriting—not an assistant's.

The note should clearly be from you. Make sure that your full name and complete address are legible—at least on the envelope. Make reference to your business association if the message will be out of context.

Mr. Johnson—

Our entire firm extends sympathy to you on the loss of your beloved wife. We have honored her memory with a donation to your neighborhood block association.

With regards,
Janice Darwin
Sherman, Sherman, & Peña

Dear Christine,

Best wishes to you and your family on the arrival of Calvin David! These flowers are from everyone at HSW.

Cordially,
Jay

23 Agendas and Minutes

Both agendas and minutes need to be brief and objective.

■ Agendas

The written agenda focuses the purpose of the meeting and the topics you expect to cover.

Use a memo. The subject line should contain all essential information:

Subject: Meeting for all sales reps with Marketing Director Tuesday, Oct. 19, 1999, from 10 A.M. PDT till noon

If necessary, provide the purpose of the meeting in an opening line.

This meeting will determine the feasibility of an employees' service center.

List the topics, beginning (if appropriate) with the approval of the minutes of the previous meeting.

If it will simplify the activities of the meeting, list reports from the chair, subcommittees, or other participants. Personally alert those reporting what their time limits will be.

List the topics with the most important first, in case time runs short and some items have to be postponed.

Attach a detailed schedule if this is to be a multisessioned conference.

Attach any informational materials so participants will have time to prepare for the meeting.

See the appendix of this book for a sample agenda.

■ Minutes of a Meeting

- Provide a heading including the name of the organization or group, "Minutes," and the complete date of the meeting.

- Give the location. Say who called the meeting to order and at what time.

- List the full names of the participants—or the approximate number of attendees for a larger meeting.

- Organize by using the agenda as it was actually followed.

- When relevant, include a brief list of points covered during discussion of each agenda item. If the minutes will be circulated as a formal record among individuals who were not present, expand on each point so that the rationale for each decision is clear.

- List the decisions reached, if any, after each agenda item. If Robert's Rules were in effect, include who offered motions and amendments and whether they were carried or rejected.

- Because you are reporting, refrain from inserting your own opinions.

- Give the time of adjournment.

- Sign "Respectfully submitted" with your name and position.

You may be asked to summarize a meeting or presentation you attended. If so, you can use the outline for "Minutes of a Meeting." Be sure to highlight the most important points brought up in the meeting.

24 INSTRUCTIONS AND DIRECTIONS

Break down instructions or directions into small, manageable steps—in the order to be followed. Give advice as you go.

■ PROVIDE BACKGROUND INFORMATION

Tell your readers what they must know before they start:

- Describe the task to be accomplished.

    This is the best way to increase the speed of your new CD-ROM drive.

- Define all unfamiliar terms.

    Grommets are the metal rims that protect the holes where the tent poles will be inserted.

- List the necessary materials and equipment.

- Indicate the steps that must be taken in advance.

    You need to know how to back up your system registry.

- Explain how to prepare the work area.

- If necessary, tell how to dress appropriately.

■ LAY OUT THE STEPS TO BE FOLLOWED

- Anticipate any possible misunderstandings.

    The ingredients listed in parentheses may be substituted without compromising the taste.

- Be careful not to combine steps or to assume that the reader will know something you haven't spelled out.

    Lubricate and clean all the gears prior to the next step.

- Use transitions to guide the reader from step to step:

    first   meanwhile   next   after   before   while   when   now

■ PROVIDE INTERMEDIATE DESCRIPTIONS

Describe how the product will look at each stage or how the worker will know the step is successful:

> At this point, the grain of the wood should be visible, but not raised.

> Now, your sales figures should appear in the graph and in the box of totals for the year.

■ EMBELLISH INSTRUCTIONS WITH ADVICE

Explain why you suggest doing a step a certain way; include safety or health advice.

> To protect your hands and to assure sanitation, wear clean, heavy-duty rubber gloves while securing the jar lids.

Be sure to define or explain terminology.

■ CHECK YOUR INSTRUCTIONS CAREFULLY

With your instructions in hand, follow each and every step. Make changes in the sequence as necessary. Then ask a colleague unfamiliar with the process to follow the instructions. Pay close attention to any gaps. Revise where a step is unclear.

25 Reports

Reports organize information, so they should be both easily understood and accurate. Tailor the content, tone, and length of a report to the intended audience.

Although the report needs to be complete, organize it to feature only the information your audience needs to know.

■ Audience

Remember that your immediate audience may not be the only audience. Some reports are filed away and later surface in a performance review, a history of the company, or a court of law. Consider these implications as you write.

■ Purpose

Reports are used routinely in business—and for a variety of purposes. Be conscious of what the report is expected to do.

- To pitch for an account
- To inform stockholders
- To record the decisions reached at a meeting
- To justify an action requiring approval

■ Tone

Most reports (except for informal ones among colleagues) require a fairly formal tone. Keep some emotional distance; withhold your personal commentary for a section on recommendations or conclusions.

- Use people's last names and titles.

- Avoid slang, sarcasm, and anger.
- Imagine this report being read aloud to a group of people.

■ BASIC ELEMENTS

GENERAL FORMAT

If you are unfamiliar with the usual style for reports in your company or industry, check with colleagues to see a few samples. Of course, you need not be hidebound by what your predecessors have done, but often, continuity of style is expected.

Will the report require artwork? graphics? book binding, spiral binding, or a folder? Will it be published electronically? The visual presentation of the report affects its reception. Seek help if necessary.

TITLE PAGE

Make certain that all the basic information is prominently and attractively featured.

- Title
- Complete date, including year
- Company name (address may be on the back cover or on the second page)
- Prepared (or edited) by (your full name; title; phone, fax, and e-mail numbers)

TABLE OF CONTENTS (FOR REPORTS OF FIVE PAGES OR MORE)

List the section headings and page numbers; for lengthy reports, list subheadings as well.

THE REPORT ITSELF

Introduction

- Include necessary background or history.
- Be sure all the main points of the report are presented briefly.

Body Paragraphs

Often a report is written in response to a request. It is your job to organize the information so that the important points are featured.

- Make sure that any questions have been answered.
- Use facts and examples to demonstrate your key points.
- Use mostly short paragraphs.

Two typical organizational patterns are covered at the end of this chapter.

Headings

Headings should be inviting but also accurate. Do one check for outline logic after you have revised and reorganized the report. Break up lengthy sections with subheadings whenever possible.

Make sure that all headings are in similar grammatical format—for example, all nouns (such as in this chapter) or all verb phrases (such as in Chapter 24, "Instructions and Directions").

Graphics

Insert illustrations, charts, and graphics within the text at the point of reference. See Chapter 8, "Adding Visual Interest."

Conclusions and Recommendations

Highlight the most important points in your conclusion, and/or list recommendations for future action.

Appendix

Supplementary information, supporting illustrations, lists of sources consulted—all go at the end of the report, with an appropriate heading for each.

Index

Lengthy reports may need an index listing topics, names of individuals, and names of companies. Most word-processing programs have a feature that will give you a good draft of an index, which you can then edit.

◼ ELECTRONIC VERSIONS

Make certain that you list the contents of even a short report at the beginning of an electronic version—preferably with links to each section so readers won't have to scroll through the entire document to reach the section they are interested in. Spend time on the formatting, design elements, and colors for the most attractive and easy reading possible.

◼ TWO COMMON TYPES OF REPORTS

Here are two outlines you can apply to writing many reports.

STUDY OF A PROBLEM

- Give the historical background.
- Explain your methodology.
- List the findings in detail, but organized by type—such as "Problems due to poor drainage," "Problems due to inadequate sanitation," and so forth.
- Label examples as such.
- Give your recommendations.

- Attach a list of sources researched, if appropriate. If you used personal interviews, be sure to include the interviews in your list—names, positions, dates interviewed, and so forth.

DESCRIPTION OF ACCOMPLISHMENTS (COMPANY REPORT OR PERSONNEL REVIEW)

- Organize the accomplishments by type.

- Arrange the types in descending order of importance.

- Within each type, list accomplishments in chronological or hierarchical order.

- Find a unifying theme to use in the introduction and conclusion, and as transition between sections.

See Chapter 5, "Organizing Your Ideas," for suggestions on how to organize sections of the report.

26 Newsletters and Press Releases

The purpose of newsletters and press releases is to both disseminate information and to enhance the company's image.

■ Newsletters

Newsletters can serve as great promotional tools outside the company; in-house, they can inform, entertain, and encourage camaraderie. Sending copies of newsletters with a personal note can give a small organization a very large image.

DEVELOP A RECOGNIZABLE FORMAT TO USE FOR EVERY ISSUE

- Make the title easy to read—test by photocopying in black and white.

- Provide all pertinent information—including the full name of the editor, the company name, complete mailing address, phone, e-mail, and fax numbers—preferably in a border on the back page.

- Date and number each issue.

WRITE FOR YOUR PRIMARY AUDIENCE, BUT KEEP OTHERS IN MIND

- Check articles for context and tone—for example, outsiders may not get your "in" jokes.

- Provide background information where necessary for outsiders.

- Identify all persons by full title or job description.

- Invite response from your audience, especially on high-interest events. Then, publish appropriate letters—with the author's permission.

USE INTERESTING LAYOUT

If you're new to layout, get some artistic advice on how to present your ideas visually and how to use the various tools now available on computers.

- Use larger, bolder typeface for headlines.

- Use columns—three are best for 8½-inch pages.

- Use subheadings and borders.

- Break up articles so that features begin on the first page and continue on a later page.

KEEP ARTICLES SHORT

- For news articles, use the news lead—*who, what, when, where, how,* and sometimes *why*—in your opening sentence.

    On May 23, 2000, Mergentime broke ground for its new headquarters in Amarillo.

- Include feature articles highlighting individuals, departments, and projects.

- When rationales or explanations must be provided, set them off with a heading or border.

- Use photographs or drawings to add interest or explanation.

PROVIDE USEFUL INFORMATION AND ANNOUNCEMENTS

Always include a "spotlight" story—a case history about a product or application or a feature on different individuals within the organization. People love to read about other people and also enjoy seeing their own names and pictures in print.

Include a calendar of upcoming events; announcements of births, weddings, and deaths in the families of employees; or interesting facts about the company's history, demographics, and successes. These items can fill blank spaces where columns run short—or you can add an attractive or entertaining graphic.

Also, don't overlook the opportunity to use the newsletter to gather information from readers—which you can then report about in a later issue. Almost everybody appreciates a piece of informal research which they haven't had time to do themselves.

ELECTRONIC VERSIONS

If your newsletter is available online, provide a sidebar with links to each current article and to related articles from previous issues. Make sure that each article includes your publication's title, e-mail and postal addresses, and the latest date of revision.

■ PRESS RELEASES

Press releases must be ready for publication. Broadcasters, local newspapers, and industry publications may be happy to use your release as is, so check every fact for accuracy; proofread thoroughly.

- Use the news lead—*who, what, when, where, how,* and sometimes *why.*

- Be brief. Editors may cut your last few paragraphs, so be sure the important information is up front. This arrangement (reverse pyramid) places less important information in each successive paragraph.

- Identify all individuals by title or position.

- Provide background information and label it as such.

- Provide a press kit, if appropriate—a folder including photographs with captions, illustrations, fact sheets, and biographical information.

See the appendix of this book for two sample press releases.

27 Proposals

In a proposal you must convince your audience about the value of what you say—to persuade them to accept your point of view.

The proposal attempts to persuade a client, a funding organization, a supervisor, or a committee that your services or project will meet their needs—often within a specified budget.

■ General Guidelines

ASSESS THE AUDIENCE

Be very clear about whether this is a receptive audience. If necessary, do some research to discover your best method for winning a positive response.

- What sorts of services are required?

- What sorts of projects has this audience supported in the past?

- Can you demonstrate a value that will persuade this audience? For example, will you provide a benefit that meets the goals of this audience?

- How are these decisions made? Will the people evaluating your proposal follow a set procedure? Is one particular person crucial to the decision?

ADOPT A PROFESSIONAL TONE

Determine the approach that will win the respect of your audience.

- Use a style that is warm and natural without assuming friendship.

- Guard against sounding desperate, cute, or intimate.

For advice on strategy, see Chapter 12, "Writing to Persuade."

SEEK ADVICE

Be sure to solicit advice from colleagues who have written successful proposals in the past. Funding organizations often have staff members assigned to advise prospective applicants; take advantage of their assistance.

■ BASIC ELEMENTS OF THE PROPOSAL

COVER LETTER

If at all possible, keep your cover letter to one page. Briefly describe what you are proposing and list the evidence you are including in your proposal.

Opening Paragraph

Summarize in a few sentences the main points of the proposal.

- What are you proposing?
- Who will benefit? How?
- Who will be involved?
- How much will it cost?
- What is the estimated time schedule?

Body Paragraphs

The middle of your cover letter will take the same points mentioned in the opening paragraph and briefly explain each. Use bullets or headings for each subtopic. Above all, remember that your goal is to persuade:

- Present the reasons why your proposal should be adopted.
- Summarize your supporting evidence.
- Highlight the most convincing facts.

Conclusion

End with a summation of the benefits of the project and, if appropriate, your desire to undertake the project.

Provide a list of the supporting materials you are attaching.

THE PROPOSAL ITSELF

Application Forms

If there is an application form that you must use, scan it if an electronic version is not available. Pay close attention to the guidelines because a technicality could eliminate you from the competition.

If No Format Is Prescribed

A good outline would include the following sections:

- Overview of the proposal
- Explanation of the problem—the goal of the proposal
- Proposed solution with factual support
- Logistics: timetable, personnel, budget
- Criteria for evaluating the project

SUBMIT THE MOST PERSUASIVE MATERIALS

Supporting evidence may include:

- A list and detailed description of all services that will be provided
- Reports of studies you or others have conducted
- Samples of previous work (portfolios, photographs, publications, videos, CD-ROMs, websites)
- Tables, charts, diagrams
- Letters and memos from colleagues

For external proposals (to clients and outside funding agencies), also include:

- Your résumé—and those of any colleagues who will be working with you

- Testimonials from previous employers or clients

For external proposals, you will need permission to reproduce material taken from outside sources, adding "reproduced by permission" after the credit line.

If you are submitting a proposal electronically, consider the advice offered at the end of Chapter 25, "Reports."

28 RÉSUMÉS

Your résumé serves as an essential tool for job hunting; once you have a job, it can be modified for promotional purposes.

The résumé and cover letter attempt to persuade a very busy employer to grant you some precious time. Your reader wants to know what skills you have that will benefit the company.

Both cover letter and résumé should make the level of your accomplishments clear, in a concise way. Save detailed documentation for the interview. If you lack experience in your chosen field, emphasize the relevant job skills you have developed.

Features of an appropriate résumé vary from field to field. Look at several résumés in your own profession for guidance.

See the Appendix of this book for a sample cover letter and four sample résumés.

■ COVER LETTER

In a job search, your résumé should always be accompanied by a cover letter (folded together, with the cover letter on top but not attached). Even if you decide to do a mass mailing as part of your search, each cover letter must be individually addressed (preferably to a name, not just to a title) and individually signed, in ink.

- The cover letter should be at most a page long. It should be readable in less than a minute.

- If you have a personal connection, mention it up front (and do everything possible to find a personal connection).

    James Stone recommended that I apply to you for the position of systems director.

- Stress how you will fit into this specific organization.

    My experience with all aspects of DataSystems technology qualifies me uniquely for supervising your planned expansion.

- Do not overlap your résumé point for point, but do stress your most important credentials for this position.

    As the enclosed résumé shows, I have shouldered increasing levels of responsibility in management information systems since earning my degree.

- Make clear your availability for interview or teleconference.

    I will be in Boston for the next two weeks at the numbers listed below, should you wish to discuss my credentials.

■ FORMAT OF THE RÉSUMÉ

To assure that your résumé will be retained, make it as brief and to-the-point as possible.

- If you can, keep your résumé to one page.

- Strive for an uncluttered, crisp look.

- List your work history by date, employer, and job title(s), with the most recent and the most impressive first. Do not list salaries.

- Feature your best points. Use headings, subtopics, and so forth.

- Make sure that headings and explanations are consistent in grammatical form and in style. See Chapter 16, "Avoiding Tangled Sentences."

- Offer to submit a portfolio or samples of your work or letters of recommendation upon request; unless they have been requested, do not attach references. Attach a photograph (head shot) only for the performing arts, entertainment, or fashion industries.

- Be sure to have your résumé available electronically.

■ CONTENTS

Your all-purpose résumé should be written so that it lists your job history. Then you can modify your résumé as needed to feature your skills and background according to the requirements of a specific position or for promotional purposes. See the appendix of this book for a sample résumé that has been modified to feature certain skills. This is the sort of résumé you would use when changing fields.

Heading At the top, either centered or arranged attractively, give your full name, complete home address, current business address only if appropriate, phone and fax numbers, and e-mail address. If you are giving a pager number, indicate that fact in parentheses—and only list it if you are vigilant about returning calls.

Objective(s) Give a brief phrase or two describing your current career goal—if you can write one appropriate to this audience. Most of the time, you can omit the objective because it is implied in your application for that particular job.

> **Objective:** to serve in a management position in the hospitality industry

> **Objective:** to affiliate with a progressive firm that will benefit from my skills as a senior architect and project manager

Reverse chronology of job history Beginning with your current job, list the dates, the name of the employer, and the job title. If the job title doesn't make the duties clear, explain them briefly, featuring the skills the prospective employer would require. Give a brief description of the company if it is not a nationally recognized one, or if you must refer to your current employer anonymously.

List of accomplishments or skills Within the list of your previous jobs, briefly describe your main strengths or outstanding accomplishments at each.

> **June 1994–present** (firm supplying the St. Louis area with personalized installation and service for intranets). On-site programmer and troubleshooter. Created, installed, and maintained personalized software for clients—many in high-data industries with systems of over 100 workstations.

Brief education history List by dates, university, and degree, followed by your major or type of study. If relevant, mention extracurricular activities. Unless you are trying to fill up the page, omit all reference to high school and earlier.

1987–91 University of Vermont BS in Computer Technology.
Dean's list. Volunteer 1988–91 (three hours weekly, twelve
weeks per semester, seven semesters) training senior citizens in
computer use. Also provided maintenance to computer systems
in local public schools.

List of references Usually, it is best to end with "references are
available upon request," but if you already have letters of
recommendation, you can list the names and titles. You may
also list the contents of your portfolio or other materials that
support your credentials.

PART
FOUR

SPECIAL PROJECTS

29 RESEARCH ON THE INTERNET

The Internet has made it possible to quickly find vast amounts of information on just about every conceivable subject. To use the Internet efficiently, however, you need to get and keep a clear idea of the exact information you are seeking.

■ BEFORE YOU PLUNGE IN

To avoid getting lost, analyze what you want before you start.

- Write down the questions you hope to answer.

- Develop a list of subtopics and synonyms that you can use as search terms in your research.

- Spend time thinking about who would know the answers. The most efficient research on the Internet is often via e-mail to the appropriate person. If you can't query the person, add that name, his or her affiliation, the area of expertise, and names of similar experts to your list of search terms.

■ CHECK A SUBJECT DIRECTORY OR SPECIALIZED DATABASE

One way to get plenty of information on your topic is to use a subject directory on the Web. For example, *Yahoo!* ⟨http://www.yahoo.com⟩ and *Lycos* ⟨http://www.lycos.com⟩ allow you to click on a category and then to click on narrower subtopics—or to type in a specific subject.

Virtual Library ⟨http://www.vlib.org/Overview.html⟩ offers a vast list of resources—and each category is maintained by an expert in that field.

Lexis-Nexis, available by subscription, indexes all news articles—including press releases and newswire articles. Although it is expensive, many organizations and public libraries are now allowing at least limited access to this service. It is definitely worth a wait in line. Use the helpline to learn how to use their very sophisticated search tools.

Many databases are now available free on the Web. For example, medical information is available from Medline ⟨www.ncbi.nlm.nig.gov/Pub/Med/⟩. Also, call the reference desk of your library for information on specialized databases for your particular topic. See addresses of other websites in the appendix of this book.

■ Use Metasearchers

If the subject directory or database doesn't yield enough information, use a metasearcher, which will search through a number of search engines simultaneously and organize the results. The same query will bring up different results from different search engines, so from the metasearcher's results you may find that one search engine is better for your topic. Metasearchers also save you time because they modify your phrases according to the rules of each specific search engine. See the appendix of this book for descriptions and addresses.

■ Use Various Combinations of Search Terms

On the screen, you will see a horizontal box outlined. Type into the box the words you want the search engine to hunt for.

Every search program uses slightly different rules of operation, but most use two searching conventions. Check the directions or helpline of the program before beginning.

- Quotation marks indicate that a phrase is to be treated as one search term—for example, "Chrysler building."

- "Boolean operators" such as *and* and *or* tell the computer how to interpret your list of search terms. In general:

and specifies that both terms should appear.

or specifies that either term should appear.

not specifies that a term should not appear.

When a search engine says that "Boolean *and* is implied," you don't need to type *and*; just type in all the terms you want with a space between them.

Some search engines use the plus sign (+) instead of *and*, and the minus sign (–) instead of *not*.

For example, information on the quality of diamonds can be found with these search terms:

diamond and carat and clarity not baseball

or

diamond+carat+clarity–baseball

As you narrow the focus of your research, use narrower combinations of terms (such as *diamond and DeBeers or Tiffany and brilliance and "white clarity"*) to get material that is more specific to your topic.

Allow time for browsing and, above all, be persistent.

■ Too Few or Too Many Listings

The most common problems that researchers experience are that they can't find any sources or that they find too many sources. In either case, first consult the helpline for that search engine.

NO MATCH FOR YOUR REQUEST

- You may have misspelled one or more words.

- You may have used the wrong symbols or phrasing for that particular search engine.

- You may need to try a different search engine or database.

- You may have submitted too narrow a search. Try generalizing a bit. For example, if one of your required terms is *"Fort Worth,"* change it to *Texas*. Once you find some sites, their links will take you to others.

- Give both the abbreviation and the full name, linked by *or* (*CIA* or *"Central Intelligence Agency"*).

- Try adding more alternatives—both more general and more specific:

    chocolate, cocoa, bittersweet, "milk chocolate," mocha, Hershey's, Godiva

- The information may be there, but your computer cannot reach it at this time. Try later.

TOO MANY LISTINGS

- Take a look at the first ten results to see if they coincide at all with your topic. For instance, if an inquiry on *"two-year-olds" and tantrums* yielded thousands of articles, and the first ten are all about horses, you'll need to rephrase the search.

- If the first ten listings are on your topic, skim a few of them to extract more search terms.

- Add more words to your search string, putting a more specific word first.

■ IMPORTANT RESOURCES

Government agencies and nonprofit organizations provide valuable statistics and other information through their websites. Use a search engine and add *"government"* to your search terms. Look for websites with *.gov* or *.org* in their addresses.

Research libraries, such as the Library of Congress and the New York Public Library, have websites that you can consult— giving you the opportunity to look at major listings of books and, in some cases, databases as well. Use a search engine to find a specific library, or check the comprehensive list at ⟨www.library.usask.ca/hywebcat/⟩.

CARL (Colorado Alliance of Research Libraries) is a service that lists scholarly articles according to subject. You can order copies of the articles for a fee or you can record the bibliographic information and find the article in your own library. To reach CARL, type in ⟨www.carl.org/carlweb⟩.

Dejanews has indexed, according to topic, the public conversations on Internet bulletin boards and newsgroups. You'll find a wide range of quality—from commercial junk to expert opinion. To reach Dejanews, type in ⟨www.deja.com⟩.

Homepages of colleges and universities can link you to libraries and course materials developed by college faculty: reading lists, syllabuses, and more. You can find these homepages through search engines. Try using the name of a particular college or your topic phrase plus "*college*," or look at the index the University of Texas has produced, arranged by subject, at ⟨www.utexas.edu/world/lecture/⟩.

■ CAUTIONS

The Internet can take up all of your research time. If you're not careful, you can easily get sidetracked by interesting but irrelevant information. Researching electronically can become a mesmerizing activity, and you might find that at the end of a pleasant afternoon there is nothing substantial to report.

Remember your angle on the topic and stick to it. Skip material that is only loosely related to your specific research questions. Again, persistence pays.

Beware of the need to evaluate information obtained on the Internet. Although there are many well-maintained and reliable websites, the quality and accuracy of statements on the Internet vary widely. Anyone can put up a website, and anyone can claim to be an authority. No one checks or credits the information in chat rooms and on most bulletin boards.

Don't overlook print materials. For many subjects, recent books and articles in print are more thorough and authoritative. Your office may already own the most important reference books

and periodicals. However, you may need to use an index at
your public library to find the articles you need. Some
publications are also available online, often for a fee.

Don't overlook other electronic media. The commercial
networks, National Public Radio, and the Public Broadcasting
System all maintain websites where you can get information
on current events as well as features.

When referring to Internet addresses, follow the conventions.
It is fine to omit the http:// in Web addresses because most
browsers add that part automatically. When the address
appears at the end of a sentence, enclose it in angle brackets,
as we have done throughout this book. Otherwise, the
period looks like part of the address.

30 CREDITING OUTSIDE SOURCES

You can often improve a report or presentation by referring to the words or ideas of others. When you do, you will need to give credit.

Although you will not ordinarily need to use the complex system of documentation required for college research papers, you will still need to identify the sources of quotations, facts, and someone else's original ideas. Crediting outside sources is more than a matter of honesty; it also:

- Lends authority to your assertions

- Demonstrates your thoroughness and knowledge

- Allows your reader to pursue the subject further

■ IN-TEXT REFERENCES

The most graceful method for giving credit to a source is to mention the author, title, and copyright date within your sentence.

Book

> Richard Tarnas in *The Passion of the Western Mind* (1991) traces what he calls the "pervasive masculinity of the Western intellectual tradition" (445) which he sees as ready at the moment for integration with the feminine and the ecological.

Notice that the page number, if you want to include it, goes in parentheses at the end of the quotation or the information, before the period. Should you prefer to put all the reference information into the parentheses, use the last name of the author and the date, followed by a comma and the page number.

> You may agree with one social critic who sees the "pervasive masculinity of the Western intellectual tradition" (Tarnas 1991, 445) as ready at the moment for integration with the feminine and the ecological.

Article

> Job security today requires being able to sell your personal skills

> rather than relying on an employer's goodwill, as Stephen M. Pollan and Mark Levine point out in *Worth* (September 1998).

(Notice that the title of the publication is cited rather than the title of the specific article.)

Internet

> T. S. Miller's posting on the *Motley Fool Message Board* ⟨http://boards.fool.com.index.html⟩(7 January 1999) provides a good analysis of the independent farmer's management of significant financial assets.

Notice that the Internet address is enclosed in angle brackets. For long Internet addresses, use a footnote. The date given is the date of last update for the site, or if that is unknown, the date you viewed it.

■ FOOTNOTES

You can use footnotes either for detailed identification of a source or for supplementary information. Footnotes are the least intrusive method of referring to sources, and word-processing programs make the formatting relatively easy.

To identify a source, include:

- Author (first name first)—if no author is listed, put the organization that created the document.

- Title (for an article, include the title of the article, in quotation marks, and the title of the publication, italicized).

- additional information, depending on the type of source.

  ~ For a book, the city of publication, publisher, and date

  > Richard Tarnas, *The Passion of the Western Mind.* New York: Ballantine, 1991.

  ~ For an article, the date and pages

  > Stephen M. Pollan and Mark Levine, "Live Rich," *Worth* September 1998. 70–80.

  ~ For a website, the date created (if available), the date you viewed it, and the complete address in angle brackets

T. S. Miller. Online posting. *Motley Fool Message Board.*
7 January 1999, 8 January 1999
⟨http://boards.fool.com.index.html⟩.

■ LIST OF REFERENCES CONSULTED

Using in-text references or footnotes should be sufficient to acknowledge sources in most business writing. However, on occasion, you may need or want to provide a list—labeled "Bibliography," "References," "Recommended Reading," "Works Cited," or "Works Consulted"—at the end of a report. Depending on how you label it, this list can be used to acknowledge background research or the sources you have cited, or to give suggestions for further reading on the topic.

Use the same format as for footnotes but with no numbers. Instead, put authors' last names first and make one alphabetical list. For each entry, indent the second and additional lines.

Note: This chapter presents a simplified version of the documentation styles recommended by the American Psychological Association, the *Chicago Manual of Style,* the Council of Biology Editors, and the Modern Language Association. Their website addresses are listed in the appendix of this book if you need to conform precisely to their individual specifications.

References

Miller, T. S., Online posting. *Motley Fool Message Board.* January 7, 1999, January 8, 1999 ⟨http://boards.fool.com.index.html⟩.

Pollan, Stephen M., and Mark Levine, "Live Rich," *Worth* September 1998. 70–80.

Tarnas, Richard, *The Passion of the Western Mind.* New York: Ballantine, 1991.

31 Recurring Projects

Much business writing falls into a few main categories and formats. Taking time to analyze how you produced what you have written makes it easier next time.

■ Develop Templates and Outlines

Save yourself time by developing templates (basic layouts in your word-processing program) for all recurring written projects. Even projects that change substantially—depending on content and audience—may follow similar outlines or processes.

Review, for example, the various kinds of letters you regularly write. Select a few well-written ones so you can develop some templates that will work for you. You might have identified these categories:

- Cover letter for contract
- Response to inquiry
- Response to proposal
- Response to job applicant
- Letter of recommendation
- Letter of complaint
- Letter requesting information

For each category, use the successful letter as your model, make a template, and label it accordingly. Make each template as detailed as possible, with as many key sentences and phrases as you can reuse.

You can develop a similar list for other types of writing you routinely do in the course of the year—such as annual reports, studies, evaluations, minutes, press releases, and so forth.

■ Keep a Notebook

As you work on a long-term or difficult project, take notes on the details of the process:

- The time schedule—particularly the length of time required by you and by others to complete each phase of the work

- The names, phone and fax numbers, and e-mail addresses of consultants

- The reason for each success

- The reason for any difficulties

- The specific characteristics of this project and this audience

- Any cautions to yourself and others for next time

■ PREPARE A TICKLER FILE

Using the details in your notebook, prepare a tickler file (a list of reminders keyed to a schedule) for each type of project. Include the following:

- A summary of the advice to yourself

- The phone/fax/e-mail/address list of helpers and consultants, and so forth

- Copies of the appropriate templates

- A copy of the last document

- A suggested basic schedule

32 Long-Term Projects

Completing a long-term project on time requires that you identify your priorities for it early on and then methodically work on these priorities at regular intervals.

■ Planning Your Project

BRAINSTORM AND FREEWRITE TO GET A SENSE OF THE PROJECT

You should identify the following:

- The topics you will be covering

- The steps you must follow

- What you already have on hand

- The information you need and how you will get it

- The people you must call

- The additional supplies, reports, graphics, and so on that you need

- Any consultants, graphic artists, printers, and so on that you need to line up

For tips on brainstorming and freewriting, see Chapter 4, "What to Do When You're Stuck."

DEVELOP A LONG-TERM PLAN FOR YOUR PROJECT

- List the steps for the project in chronological order.

- Estimate the amount of time each step requires. Be very realistic—and generous—allowing time for delays and unforeseen disasters.

- Develop a series of deadlines for yourself—including time for some breaks.

- Make a schedule for any consultants, collaborators, or outside jobbers, and ensure their commitments.

WRITE A TENTATIVE OUTLINE OR TABLE OF CONTENTS

Using your brainstorming and freewriting, develop a rough plan for the written product.

◼ DURING THE PROJECT

KEEP A NOTEBOOK—EITHER ON PAPER OR ELECTRONICALLY

Begin writing as soon as you can—out of order, any time that you think of something to say. In your notebook, keep copies of your schedule and your tentative outline, and revise them as necessary.

It's also a good idea to keep a section of your notebook just for notes to yourself. These notes should be about your sense of the project and where it is leading. Periodically, review what you have written and adjust the working document.

NETWORK

Talk about your project with others. Over time, people can offer you information or advice if they think you'd welcome it. Schedule frequent meetings (at least by phone) with your associates, supervisor, or client. One problem with long-term projects is that they can be isolating. Discuss your project with friends—not so much to get their ideas as to articulate your own.

IF YOU NEED TO DO RESEARCH, BEGIN RIGHT AWAY

Gather information or conduct your study as soon as possible. Write up your findings as you go. Maintain a separate "clippings" file for the project and drop into it any bits of related information you might find useful at a later date.

USE YOUR OUTLINE TO ORGANIZE FILES INTO THE COMPUTER

Using your outline or table of contents, name a file for each topic. As soon as you can, write a detailed outline, tentative notes, or a very rough draft in each file. What is important at first is to get something approximately close to what you want to say. Don't strive for perfection. You will expand or develop as you get further into the project.

PLAN TO REVISE A NUMBER OF TIMES

- Put your work into a computer early in the process and store it in short documents rather than one long one.

- Large projects in particular go through more drafts than you might expect. Strive to have a rough draft of every part of the project halfway through your allotted time schedule, then revisit the parts to expand, revise, and fine-tune.

- Revision will entail not only touch-ups but complete changes of emphasis. Allow more time proportionately for revising a long project than you usually do for the revision process.

■ As the Deadline Approaches

- Make sure that you have communicated whatever you require from others and that they are on schedule.

- Revise your outline if necessary and use it to format the entire document. Add headings and bullets so subtopics are clearly distinguished from main topics.

- Add a table of contents and index if needed.

- Go through the entire finished product several times, checking each time for just one aspect:

  ~ **Accuracy** Of facts, numbers, quotations, and so forth

  ~ **Completeness** No unanswered questions or unsupported assertions

~ **Readability** Plenty of headings, a layout that showcases your main points, brief paragraphs, and well-constructed sentences

~ **Correctness** Of grammar, punctuation, vocabulary, etc.

33 Collaborative Projects

In the professional world, you'll probably find yourself involved in a variety of collaborative projects.

■ General Principles for Working in a Group

LET GO OF TOTAL CONTROL

Be open to the variety of ways different people contribute. Some people like to take charge and immediately have an idea of what to do. Some are quiet but do excellent work. Some add fun and life to the process. Some care about getting details right. Some are eager to help with the basics—keyboarding, for instance.

Negative criticism causes not only bad feelings but poor work. Avoid being picky; often a problem which bothers you will get solved in the course of discussion. An idea that at first sounds out of line could be important. Stay positive toward each member of the group, give each person time to speak, and the group will work far more creatively, happily, and successfully.

EXERCISE PATIENCE

People work at different rates. To benefit from the whole group, fast workers shouldn't rush those whose ideas need time.

Realize that time "wasted" is not always wasted. Exchanging news, having coffee, arguing over the same point twice is not really wasting time. These processes are how a group becomes a team, and more of the group become involved. To work well in a group, you need to tolerate some degree of chaos.

■ Tips for Writing Collaboratively

Agree on intermediate deadlines. Decide together when everyone will bring a certain amount of work to discuss. Even when you intend to divide the writing of the final report, seeing each other's work at key points will help you to unify the project and use everyone's ideas.

Write separately, in most cases, then come together. The style and continuity are often disastrous when you compose sentences together. Revise as a group, but recognize that good revision takes time. The group needs to talk until you discover what you really want to say.

Circulate one copy of the final draft. Everyone should write comments at the appropriate place in the document—always identifying themselves by initials—either

- In ink on the page
- On sticky notes
- On the electronic copy in brackets

Put one person in charge of the final manuscript. This writer will make sure the style of different parts is consistent and correct. A number of people should double-check the final copy.

■ SOME TIPS FOR WORKING IN A GROUP

Here are some practical steps that a group can take from the outset to ensure that they work together smoothly and effectively:

Take advantage of having a group to work with. Meet regularly and frequently to exchange ideas and to help each other. Make sure that the group is functioning well—that no one is dominating and that no one is left out.

Agree in advance about how the group will handle conflict and disagreements. At first, the whole group is usually excited about the project; then, the inevitable disagreements, personality conflicts, and work-style clashes begin to seep in. Plan for the storm ahead of time by agreeing to immediately, openly, and honestly bring the problem before the group. Stay away from gossip and backbiting—handle each conflict as it arises before it becomes severe.

Decide on the division of labor. Talk over how each group member works, and what each does best and likes to do. List all necessary steps and then let people volunteer. Make sure that the group reviews the final list so that everyone feels that the division of work is both fair and practical.

Decide on who will be speaking for the group. Designate one person for contact or follow-through with outsiders. This responsibility can be divided up, but for example, the same person should be working with the graphics department each time—and the group should agree on what will be said.

Decide how you will handle expenses. Your expenses may be automatically absorbed without outlay of either money or paperwork. Or, you may have a limited budget and additional expenses will not be covered. If necessary, make a list of expenses you know you will incur during the project—and then add a small sum for unexpected expenses. All members must agree on the expenses ahead of time. If receipts must be submitted for reimbursement, decide whether one person will take charge or whether everyone will submit for reimbursements individually.

Be flexible. Be prepared to modify the original plan if it is not working. For example, one member may have been working harder and longer than anyone else with not much to show for it. The whole group might decide that this person needs help or that this part of the project needs to be reconsidered.

34 THE SPOKEN WORD

Spoken errors are usually overlooked in conversations, but when you are giving a formal talk or presentation, be sure to keep your words error-free.

These suggestions apply to both broadcast and platform presentations:

- Be certain your grammar is correct—particularly verb agreement and pronoun usage.

- Vary the rhythm of your sentences.

- Use active verbs.

- Use concrete language.

- Stay away from phrases that are offensive, sarcastic, or trendy. If in doubt, don't say it.

- Make contact with your audience and with other participants.

■ PREPARATION

Prepare an outline with brief reminders of examples or anecdotes. Consider writing out an important speech in its entirety. In some cases, you may need to provide a copy for the record anyway, and writing it out helps you to craft better sentences. Check it first by reading it aloud, but plan to use the outline for your presentation.

Don't plan to read your speech. If you must have the entire speech with you for a sense of confidence, boldface and enlarge the headings so you can glance at them and extemporize on the details. You'll kill your presentation if you face your notes instead of your audience.

Practice your speech. You may find it helpful to stand in front of a mirror. Picture your audience—including any specific people you know. Use appropriate, modulated gestures and facial expressions. Enunciate clearly. Note where you stumble over the phrasing and simplify those parts. Use plain English.

Practice with any visuals you intend to use. Mark the points in the outline of your speech where you will be using the visuals. If possible, practice with the exact equipment you will be using.

Time yourself. Allow for whatever your habit usually is—do you speed up or slow down when onstage? Mark on your outline what points you can cut or expand upon—depending on how your allotted time is going. Especially in a broadcast, you cannot come up too short or go beyond your time limit. Planning ahead will prevent sudden panic.

■ PRESENTATION

Bring a list of key points. Highlight the points you want to cover, and arrange them in order of importance. If others are controlling the agenda, make sure that your most important point is addressed as soon as appropriate.

Dress appropriately. Wear neutral or soft colors; avoid complicated patterns and garish or noisy jewelry. Wear light blue, not a white shirt for television.

Insert a slight pause before you talk. For broadcasts and teleconferences, this regular pause will allow for any lag in transmission time. It also gives you an advantage when you need to pause in response to a tough question; the pause will be part of your rhythm.

Take brief notes (in one or two words) during the discussion in a platform panel or teleconference. This way, you can modify your planned presentation in reaction to others. Panel presentations and teleconferences—even formal ones—should operate as conversations.

Don't interrupt others—no matter how tempting. Even if you're correct in what you say, you will draw unfavorable attention to yourself.

Don't read!

35 EDITING OTHER PEOPLE'S DRAFTS

Whether you are collaborating or supervising, there may be times when you must offer advice on how to improve a draft.

■ ASSESSING THE DOCUMENT AS A WHOLE

Before you read the document, determine the time available for making changes and assess its relative importance—to the author and to the organization. Ask the writer what help is needed.

Be tactful. No one likes to feel criticized. If possible, read the document out of the author's presence. Don't over-edit.

Read the entire document through to get a sense of its logic and style:

- What is the point?

- What is the sequence of ideas? Look for gaps in reasoning and missing information.

- Consider the writer's point of view—Is there something you know that the writer needs to know?

- Identify the strengths and well-written parts.

- If you see errors in punctuation, spelling, or grammar, can they be categorized and described globally?

If you can, discuss this initial reaction with the author before making any written comments. Often, the help that is needed is with organization, and this can best be done in discussion—before the actual editing. In this conversation, listen for any additional points the author mentions that should be included. Reserve minor details for later. The author may want to revise the document before you comment further.

■ Editing on the Document Itself

Avoid the school teacher stance!

> **Begin with as much praise as possible.** Give a general comment that covers the good parts first and then what needs to be changed.

> **Make as few marks as possible on the printed words.** Instead, write comments in the margin. Phrase your comments as questions whenever you can. Underline or highlight a passage that you recommend be revised. If corrections are necessary, use a colored pen (not black) to make neat, small changes that are easy to see.

> **Suggest alternate phrasing where possible.** The author may be unaware of a better way to present an idea.

> **Refer the writer to sections of this book that will be helpful.** Give appropriate page numbers to save the author time.

36 Writing for Others

When asked to write material (a letter or speech) that someone else will sign or present, be very clear about what you have been asked to do.

■ CLARIFYING THE REQUEST

Before you leave your colleague's office, be sure you know the answers to the following questions:

Freedom Have you been given freedom to write this however you wish, or will you need to get approval?

Information What help or information will you need?

Deadline Have you been given a realistic deadline? If you see a time crunch ahead, tell your colleague immediately.

Purpose Is the document intended to be persuasive or informative?

Audience Who will read (or hear) it? The audience will determine the tone. Ask for guidance if you're unsure.

Length and format Is the expected length rough or exact? Is there a model for the format desired?

■ WRITING A SPEECH FOR ANOTHER

When writing a speech for someone else to deliver, strive for an easy delivery, with a tone appropriate to the content—preferably in the style of the speaker.

Read it aloud.

- Simplify places where you stumble; change parts where you find yourself rephrasing.

- Build in pauses for dramatic delivery.

- Be sure, above all, that it is absolutely correct—both in content and mechanics.

PART
FIVE

CORRECTNESS: USAGE

■ A WORD ABOUT CORRECTNESS

Too much concern about correctness can inhibit your writing, so defer the fear of errors until you have your first draft. On the other hand, recognize that basic errors in writing can cost you prestige, time—and even money. We encourage you to master the few rules presented here as quickly as possible so that you can feel secure about your writing. Once that happens, you'll be free to concentrate on what you want to say.

37 CONFUSING WORDS

Spell checkers won't help you when you correctly spell the wrong word.

accept	To take, to receive
	This office does not accept collect phone calls.
except	Not including
	Laundry products—except for ours—leave an invisible film that attracts dirt.
affect	To change or influence
	Casual encounters in the office can affect morale.
effect	The result, the consequence
	Effect is usually a noun, so you'll find *the* or *an* in front.
	Social scientists have studied the effects of noise levels on productivity in the workplace.
allusion	Reference, what was alluded to
	Kiki's allusion to last year's private negotiations was inappropriate.
delusion	Fantasy
	He is under the delusion that the vice president is his buddy.
elision	Omission
	Your elision—whether by computer error or neglect—cost us the contract.
illusion	Dream, artificial image
	The projector creates an illusion of snow falling.
an	Use before words starting with vowels or pronounced as if they did (*an age, an egg, an hour, an M&M*). Use a before words starting with consonant sounds or long *u* (*a bat, a coat, a union*).
bare	Exposed, to uncover
	Protect your bare back with sunscreen.

Please bare your wrist so we can measure it for the watchband.

bear	The animal; to carry (past tense, *bore*; past participle, *borne*)

I do not intend to bear the responsibility for this project single-handedly.

Scott bore up well during that brutal press conference.

Prior to this pregnancy, the patient has borne four children without complications.

brake	The mechanism that stops the engine; to halt any motion.

Let's put the brakes on this spending trend.

Brake on the approach, accelerate on the curve.

break	A separation; to shatter or separate into pieces or parts

After the break, we will resume the negotiations.

Let's break for dinner.

Don't break the seal if you plan to return the software.

conscience	The sense of right and wrong

Mr. Bradstreet claims to have a clear conscience regarding the distribution of bonuses.

conscious	Aware

We became conscious of the need to widen our market.

desert	Arid country (accent on the first syllable); to abandon (accent on the second syllable)
deserts	What one deserved—good or bad; always plural (accent on the second syllable)

After three days in the desert, the cinematographer deserted the project. That is just deserts for the ad executive who decided to schedule the shoot in August.

dessert	The sweet portion of the meal (accent on the second syllable)

We will feature an article on frozen desserts.

etc.   Abbreviation of *et cetera* (Latin for "and so forth"). "And so forth" is preferable. However, don't use "and etc."—which means "and and so forth."

For a nominal fee, we can personalize the paper goods for your office party (table runners, napkins, beverage containers, etc.).

flower   Blossom, to flourish

The children's art program is flowering in surprising ways.

flour   Ground grain or nuts

Use semolina flour for making pasta.

good, well   *Well* can refer to one's health (an adjective) or to the way one performs (an adverb). *Good* is always an adjective, referring to having better quality.

Barbara Withers supervises well.

Ms. Withers is a good supervisor.

But note these tricky cases:

Olivia looks good. (She's good-looking.)

Rivka looks well. (She's no longer sick.)

Clara sees well. (Her eyes work.)

hoard   To store

horde   Large, often unruly group

The script requires the old woman to hoard her jewelbox in the cave as the hordes of soldiers cross the river.

it's   *It is.* Test by substituting "it is."

It's finished. It's time to go.

its   Possessive

Every goat is attached to its own legs.

The pharmacy closed its doors December 1st.

[No apostrophe. *It is* cannot be substituted.]

lay	To put something down
	-ing: Tim is laying the report in the chairman's hands at this very moment.
	Past tense: *laid*
	Tim laid the report on the chairman's desk early this morning.
	Once you *lay* something down, it *lies* there.
lie	To recline, to stay down; also, to tell a lie
	The new binding will allow the opened book to lie flat.
	Past tense (here's the tricky part): *lay*
	The report lay unnoticed under the tea tray.
	[*Lied* always means "told a lie."]
lying	Reclining
	The lion was lying under the shrubs, as directed.
	Telling a lie
	Unfortunately, our supplier was lying about the delivery date.
lead	A metal (rhymes with *red*); to provide direction (rhymes with *reed*)
	Place a lead apron over the patient's body during dental X rays.
	Mr. Casey leads the sales force—surpassing his quota each quarter.
led	Past tense of *lead*
	Ms. Salina led the department in this year's fund raiser.
loose	Not tight
	After Helene dieted for two weeks, her shoes and rings were loose.
lose	To misplace
	Please call this number if you lose your password.

	To be defeated
	I win; you lose.
of, have	Could have, should have, would have—not would of
passed	An exam, a car, a football; also passed away (died)
	This moisturizer has passed the most stringent dermatological tests.
past	Yesterdays (the past; past events); also, beyond
	Our past accomplishments are good predictors of success.
	Those policies were corrected in the past.
	Our office is two miles past the railroad tracks.
pore	Opening in covering or skin; to study carefully
	Minuscule pores in this fabric provide comfort during exercise.
	I expect you to pore over every aspect of the report before Monday.
pour	To transfer out by tipping the container; heavy rainfall
	We've been pouring funds into this project with no visible results.
quiet	Spike Jones rarely played quiet music.
quit	The lighting designer did not quit work until 2 A.M.
quite	Hippos are quite fast, considering their bulk.
sole	solitary, the only one; a fish
soul	spirit; soul food, soul music
	Catfish, not sole, is better for this soul food recipe.
	The sole survivor of the riot remains in a coma.
than	Comparison
	Mr. Hacz is more skillful with facts and figures than with people.

then	Next
	Make certain that the primary coat is thoroughly dry; then, apply the first coat of color.
their	Something is theirs. (One way to remember: Heirs own things.)
	The employees rate their flexible hours as the primary benefit.
there	A place: Go over there. (All the place words end in *-ere*.)
	There is . . . There are . . . There was . . . There were
	There are several alternatives to Ms. Verona's offer.
they're	They are.
	They're trying hard to be polite.
to	Direction
	Give it to me.
	Go to New York.
	A verb form
	To see, to run, to be
	(Note that you barely pronounce *to*.)
too	More than enough
	Too hot, too bad, too late, too much.
	Also
	Me, too!
	(Note that you pronounce *too* clearly.)
two	2
ware	utility items, gear
	Vacuum cleaner salespeople used to sell their wares door-to-door.
	Some hardware stores now sell software and underwear as well.

wear	What one puts on one's body; what happens with use
	Wear different shoes on alternate days to avoid wearing them out too soon.
were	Past tense
	You were, we were, they were.
we're	We are
	We're a nation of immigrants.
where	A place
	Where are the prototypes now?
whether	If (not weather—rain or snow)
	Please let me know whether you can meet the new deadline.
who's	Who is
	Who's there?
	Who's coming with us?
whose	Possessive
	Whose diamond is this?
woman	One person
	Hannah Productions hired a woman for the job.
	a woman; a man
women	Several of them
	More and more women fly their own planes.
your	Belonging to you
	Use only for your mail, your job, and so on.
	I did not receive your message yesterday.
	Your cannot be used when you mean "you are."
you're	You are.
	I'd like to know what you're thinking.

38 ONE WORD OR TWO?

If you can put another word between, keep them separate. Otherwise, check this list.

---

all ready
The storyboards are all ready for the presentation.

They are all completely ready.

already
The agents have already taken their percentage.

all right
(always written separately)

It's all right with the client to schedule delivery for next week.

(*Alright* is not an acceptable spelling.)

a long
The last confrontation required a long time to resolve.

along
Our journey will take us along the Natchez Trace.

a lot
We owe you a lot—a whole lot.

(*A lot* is always written as two words, not to be confused with *allot*—meaning "to allocate.")

a part
We found that Ms. Velasquez was a part of every project—a significant part.

apart
Disconnect the fan before you take it apart for cleaning.

at least
(always written separately)

You'll need at least three disks to back up this program.

each other
(always written separately)

When assigning team members, consider how they've worked with each other before.

even though
(always written separately)

She will run again for office even though she has never won an election.

everybody	Jimmy's comments incensed everybody in the chat room.
	But: Every body was given a decent burial.
every day	It rains every day, every single day.
everyday	There is a difference between dress-down and everyday clothes.
every one	Every one of the associates will be eligible for the bonus.
everyone	Everyone likes pizza.
in fact	(always written separately)
	In fact, the real truth never came out.
in order	(always written separately)
	I paid the bill ahead of time in order to avoid confusion.
in spite of	(always written separately)
	We exceeded our sales quotas in spite of a reduction in personnel.
intact	I recommend that we keep the mailroom team intact.
into	Pour the batter into the heated and buttered popover pan.
in touch	(always written separately)
	Stay in touch via e-mail.
itself	(always written together)
	The snake wrapped itself around the boy's arm.
myself	I promised myself that we'd never ask such sacrifices of our people again.
	But: My self respect was at stake.
nobody	Nobody knows how Rebecca Fraser manages to juggle so many problems so cheerfully and so successfully.

	But: No body in the temporary morgue has been identified.
no one	No one on the current staff speaks Spanish.
nowadays	(always written together)
	Nowadays, you don't hear the word "icebox."
nevertheless	(always written together)
	Nevertheless, we expect the merger to be approved.
somehow	(always written together)
	The package was somehow shipped to Mississippi instead of Minnesota.
some time	You will need some time to adjust to the new schedule.
sometimes	Sometimes, I wonder why I continue to work.
throughout	(always written together)
	The research assistant was kept busy throughout the entire summer.
whenever	(always written together)
	The mood lightens whenever that CD is played.
whereas	(always written together)
	We can change colors at little expense, whereas changes in lighting will be prohibitive.
wherever	(always written together)
	People flock to him wherever he goes.
withhold	(always written together)
	Until the roof has been repaired, we will withhold the rent.
without	(always written together)
	Several days passed without a glimmer of sunlight.

39 SPELLING

There's no getting around it. Correct spelling of words in English takes patience. However, you can save time by learning the rules—particularly for those words a spell check won't catch.

◼ *I* BEFORE *E*

Use *I* before *E*
Except after *C*
Or when sounded like *A*
As in *neighbor* and *weigh.*

believe	deceive	freight
friend	receive	vein
piece	conceit	

Exceptions:

weird	foreign	leisure	seize	their

◼ WORD ENDINGS

The quiet *-ed* endings

Three *-ed* endings are not always pronounced clearly, but they need to be written.

used to	supposed to	prejudiced

-sk and *-st* endings

When *s* is added to words like these, it isn't always clearly pronounced, but it still needs to be there.

asks	consists	psychologists
risks	insists	scientists
desks	suggests	terrorists
tasks	costs	interests

The *-y* endings

- When a verb ends in *y*, keep the *y* when you add *ing*. To add *s* or *ed*, change the *y* to *i*.

crying	cries	cried
studying	studies	studied
trying	tries	tried

- When a noun ends in *y*, make it plural by changing the *y* to *i* and adding *es*.

activities	families	theories

Exception: Simply add *s* to nouns ending in *ey*.

attorneys	monkeys	valleys

p or *pp*? *t* or *tt*?

Listen to the vowel before the added part.

- If the vowel is long (sounds like its own letter name), use only one consonant:

writer	writing

The *i* in *writer* sounds like the name of the letter *i*, so use only one *t*.

- If the vowel before the added part is short (has a different sound from its name), double the consonant:

written

The *i* sounds like the *i* in *it*, so you double the *t*.

The same method works for *hoping* and *hopping*. Listen for the different sounds of the letter *o*.

Here are some other examples:

beginning	dropping	quitting
stopped	occurred	referred

An exception: *coming*

■ WORDS WITH PREFIXES AND SUFFIXES

When you add a prefix or suffix, you usually keep the spelling of the root word.

misspell	suddenness	dissatisfaction
hopeful	disappear	government
unnoticed	environment	

The -*ly* endings also follow this rule.

really   totally   lonely   finally   unfortunately

But *truly* does not follow the rule.

Exception: The final *e* is usually dropped before a suffix that starts with a vowel.

debatable   sensible   lovable

■ TRICKY WORDS

Look hard at the middle of each word:

definitely   embarrass   usually
separate   accommodate   necessary
repetition   probably   familiar
opinion   interest

40 CAPITALIZATION

Capitalize the first letter of every sentence and of names of people, organizations, localities, days of the week, and months. Do not capitalize for emphasis.

■ DO CAPITALIZE

- Names or initials of people, companies, departments, and organizations

    Tenants and Neighbors Coalition

    B.B. Thornton

    FDA (Federal Drug Administration)

    Zizzo Corporation

- Business or family names like *Group, Agency, Firm, Mother,* or *Grandfather* only when used as a name or with a name

    The Public Interest Research Group has organizations in just about every state.

    I will be happy to meet with a representative from your firm Tuesday morning.

    This is the biscuit recipe Aunt Adelaide would have used sixty years ago.

    Please forward your résumé to our Human Resources Department.

- People's titles when they precede their names

    Dr. Judd   Vice President Jan Peters   Major Gross

- Days of the week, months of the year

    Wednesday   February

- Brand names

    Kleenex   Coca-Cola   Domino's Pizza

- Public holidays

    Thanksgiving   Fourth of July

- The entire name of a specific place, event, and so on

  Oak Street   Battle of Gettysburg   Calhoun High School

- In titles, the first word, major words, and words of five letters or more

  Die Broke   "A Rose for Emily"

  Around the World in Eighty Days   *All Things Considered*

  "If the Devil Danced in Empty Pockets, He'd Have a Ball in Mine"

■ DO NOT CAPITALIZE

- Words for business or relationships like *firm, committee, department, boss, sister* after *the, a, my, his, her, their, our, your*

  our department head   your firm   her brother

  the real estate business   the organization

  My agency hopes to hire three programmers this month.

- Titles of people separate from their names, unless the title is used in lieu of a (perhaps unknown) name.

  We will hire a new marketing vice president in January.

  The Vice President for Human Resources must attend every negotiating session.

- Seasons of the year

  spring   autumn

- Generic names

  facial tissues   soda pop   pizza

- Private celebrations

  birthday   anniversary

- A type of place, event, and so on

  a dark street   the eve of battle   high school

- For emphasis

  Do not capitalize whole words (AMNESIA); do not capitalize an entire agenda or Internet message.

41 ABBREVIATIONS AND NUMBERS

Abbreviations and numbers must be clear and easily read.

■ ABBREVIATIONS

As a general rule, don't use abbreviations in formal documents. Abbreviate freely in informal messages—as long as the abbreviation is unambiguous.

FORMAL DOCUMENTS

Avoid abbreviating words within your sentences when writing formally. Particularly avoid such abbreviations as these:

Dept.   VP   thru   Co.

Do abbreviate the company name or repeated technical terms after fully spelling them out first. Do not use periods after such abbreviations.

> Widget Productions Incorporated has always been proud of quality control, so we are doubly embarrassed about your defective corkscrew. In addition to a replacement, WPI is pleased to send you two decorative wine stoppers.

Always abbreviate common titles with proper names:

Mr. Smithers   Ms. Pendergrast   St. Bartholomew

Abbreviate *doctor* only before a name:

the doctor   Dr. Salk

Do not abbreviate most other titles—whether preceding or following the name:

Vice President Witherspoon

Margery Jamieson, Associate Editor

INFORMAL DOCUMENTS

In informal communications (such as e-mail and in-house notes to colleagues), conventional abbreviations, including technical terms used in your industry, are acceptable, even preferable.

> The meeting with all DAs is scheduled for 10 A.M. Thurs. Apr. 22.

Avoid abbreviating a word that might be misinterpreted.

> Please discuss the rev. with James. (review? revision?)

■ Numbers

SPELL OUT

- Numbers that take only one or two words

  > nine   twenty-seven   two billion

- Numbers that begin a sentence

  > One hundred four years ago the ship sank.
  >
  > The ship sank 104 years ago.

- Numbers that form a compound word

  > a two-year-old baby

- Fractions

  > one-half

USE NUMERALS FOR

- Numbers that require three or more words

  > 1,889   162

- Dates, page references, room numbers, statistics, addresses, percentages, and dollars and cents

  > May 6, 1974   7,500 residents   99.44%
  >
  > page 2   221 B Baker Street $5.98

- A list or series of numbers

  > 1, 4, 9, 16, 25
  >
  > seats 12, 14, and 16

42 CORRECT PRONOUNS

I, she, he, we, they, and *who* identify the persons doing the action. *Me, her, him, us, them,* and *whom* identify the persons receiving the action.

■ PAIRS: MY PARTNER AND I/ MY PARTNER AND ME

- With a pair of people, try the sentence without the other person:

    Carter gave the account to my partner and me.
    (Carter gave the account to me, not to I.)

    The client had already sent my colleagues and me her deposit.
    (She sent . . . me her deposit, not she sent . . . I her deposit.)

    The same rule goes for *him, her, he, she.*

    The producer met with Carolyn and her.
    (The producer met with her, not with she.)

- Don't be afraid of *me;* it's often right.

    Between you and me, Kevin is in over his head.
    (Not Between you and I . . .)

    Don't use *myself* when *me* will do.

    I did the graphics myself.
    (Here, *me* cannot be substituted.)

    Sam did the graphics for Toby and me.
    (Not . . . for Toby and myself.)

■ COMPARISONS

- Use *I, he, she, we, they* when comparing with the subject of the sentence—usually the first person in the sentence.

    Ms. Jason was less responsible for supervising Sarah than I was.

    Mr. Schultz is more easily distracted than she is.

    Sometimes *is* or *was* is left off the end:

    Mr. Schultz is more easily distracted than she.

- Use *me, him, her, us, them* when comparing with the receiver, the object of the sentence—usually the person mentioned later in the sentence.

    The quality of the software is less important to John's team than to us.

Note the difference:

    The judge listened more carefully to Agnes than me.
    (The judge listened more carefully to Agnes than to me.)

    The judge listened more carefully to Agnes than I.
    (The judge listened more carefully to Agnes than I did.)

■ WHO/WHOM

- Use *whom* after prepositions (to whom, of whom, for whom, from whom, with whom).

    To whom should I address my complaint?

- Use *who* for subjects of verbs.

    Who should I say is calling?

When you're in doubt, *who* is usually acceptable.

- Use *who* for people—not *which*.

    The runner who finished last got all the publicity.

43 CONSISTENT PRONOUNS

Make a conscious choice of your pronouns. Don't shift from *a person* to *they* to *you* to *I.*

■ THE SINGULAR/PLURAL PROBLEM: *THE CUSTOMER . . . THEIR*

In common speech, we often use *they* or *their* to refer back to a singular noun.

> The customer should get their money back, no questions asked.
>
> If a person wants to succeed in real estate, they should come to our seminar.
>
> Unless someone has a strong background in music, they won't understand this project.

The customer, a person, and *someone* are singular; *they* and *their* are plural. Although you will hear this usage in conversation and will even see it in print, it is still not acceptable in most writing.

If you keep the singular noun, you will need a singular pronoun. Here are your options.

He, he or she

The old-fashioned pronoun choice to accompany *a person* or *someone* is *he:*

> Unless someone has a strong background in music, he won't understand this project.

This choice, however, presumes that *a person* is male. It should be avoided because it is sexist language. *He or she* is possible, but not if it comes several times in a row; *he or she,* when repeated, becomes clunky and awkward. Avoid *he/she* and *s/he.*

> When a person is not afraid of criticism, he or she will not worry about what others think of him or her.

One

One means *a person*—singular.

> If one wants to succeed in real estate, one should come to our seminar.

The problem here is that *one* sounds stuffy in American English. How many times can one say *one* before one makes oneself sound silly?

FOUR SOLUTIONS

A real person

Often, your best choice is to use a true-to-life example, a real person:

> Marc Frontenac hoped to succeed in real estate; after taking our seminar, his business doubled.

A real example not only makes the grammar correct, but it is also much more interesting and memorable. *A person* and *someone* are nobodies.

Plural

Instead of *the customer,* use *customers;* instead of *a person* or *someone,* try *people,* which fits with *they.*

> The customers should get their money back, no questions asked.

> If people want to succeed in real estate, they should come to our seminar.

You

You is uncomplicated and inviting when you are generalizing.

> If you want to succeed in real estate, you should come to our seminar.

> If you don't have a background in music, you won't be able to understand this project.

No pronoun

Many times, you can avoid the problem entirely by recasting the sentence.

> Anyone who wants to succeed in real estate should come to our seminar.

■ Slippery Pronouns: *You, I, We*

Writers often get tangled up in their pronouns when trying to avoid *I* or *you*. However, using *I* or *you* makes for strong writing—particularly in letters and memos.

You

Of course, *you* is best for directly addressing your reader or listener. The problem with *you* comes when you find yourself sliding back and forth between *you* and other pronouns.

> I have several concerns over Mr. Jerrold's performance. When a crisis arose, you suddenly could not locate him.

Here, the writer says *you*, but really means *I* and should say so:

> Whenever a crisis arose, I rarely could find him.

In any case, check for inconsistency and choose the best pronoun.

I

Don't be afraid of *I* if that's who you mean. In the right place, *I* has both warmth and the ring of truth.

> I am convinced that reducing staff now will hurt us in the long run.

> I have no hesitation in recommending Cynthia Jackson to you as an outstanding candidate for the position of advertising director.

We

We is appropriate when you are speaking for your company, your department, or your working group; it can also be used to mean people in general. *We* sometimes has more authority than just plain *I* and has the advantage of deflecting criticism or blame from any one person.

> We see no problem in continuing to use the incinerator we have now.

> We recommend a 10 percent increase in price immediately.

Be careful when you use *we* that you mean more than just yourself; using *I* might be more appropriate and honest.

44 PRONOUNS: AVOIDING VAGUENESS

Certain pronouns—*which, it, this,* and *that*—must refer to a single word, not to a whole phrase. Keep them near the word they refer to; eliminate them where you can.

These words are used loosely in conversation, but in most writing you should use them more precisely.

Which

Which causes the most trouble of the four. Often, it can be eliminated.

> *Imprecise:* Last month's sales offset the previous month's decline by 21 percent, which means projections for the year are holding.

> *Precise:* Last month's sales offset the previous month's decline by 21 percent; the net result means projections for the year are holding.

Use *in which* only when you mean that one thing is inside the other:

> The canisters in which we store nitrogen dioxide are leaking.

Which cannot start a sentence unless it asks a question.

It, this, or that

When you use *it,* make sure the reader knows what *it* is. When *this* or *that* seems unclear, add a noun, such as this *product* or that *outcome.*

> *Imprecise:* You need to bring the revised contracts, the presentation materials, and sixteen copies of your own report. It's urgent!

> *Precise:* We urgently need the revised contracts, the presentation materials, and sixteen copies of your own report.

Imprecise:	The focus group preferred design No. 601 for the eye shadow containers; the lowest bid is for $250 per 100 count. This means we can proceed.
Precise:	The focus group preferred design No. 601 for the eye shadow containers; the lowest bid is for $250 per 100 count. These positive results mean we can proceed.
Imprecise:	We are not paid well and receive inadequate benefits, but I don't think that we can discuss that yet.
Precise:	We are not paid well and receive inadequate benefits, but I don't think that we can discuss benefits yet.

45 VERBS: AGREEMENT WITH SUBJECTS

No matter how far apart, the subject and verb must agree. The word before the verb is not always its subject. Look for who or what is doing the action.

- Two singular subjects joined by *and* (for example, *the cologne* and *the aftershave*) make a plural and need a plural verb.

    The cologne and the aftershave complement each other.

    The morning shift coordinator and the afternoon maintenance supervisor have not agreed to the new schedule.

- Sometimes an insertion separates the subject and verb.

    The juice blend, not the other beverages, needs chilling.

    The lady who sells flowers has a mysterious voice.

- The subject cannot be the word that directly follows *of;* read the sentence without the prepositional phrase.

    One of the accountants was lenient on entertainment expenses.
    (*One* is the subject, not *accountants.*)

    Each of us accepts responsibility for the delay.

    The use of acupuncture needles has tripled.

- The subject of the sentence <u>follows</u> *there was, there were, there is, there are.*

    There is an embarrassing typo in the auto mechanics' manual.
    (*Typo* is the subject.)

    There were two causes for this power failure.
    (*Causes* is the subject.)

- Words with *one* and *body* are singular.

    Everyone agrees that the warranty was poorly written.

    Somebody always overheats the copying machine.

- Sometimes a group can be singular.

    My family does not eat crowder peas.

    In some states the jury elects the foreman.

A thousand dollars is a lot of money to carry around.

- *-ing* phrases are usually singular.

    Dating two people is tricky.

46 VERBS: CONSISTENT TENSES

Sometimes you may find yourself slipping back and forth between present and past verb tenses. Be consistent, especially within each paragraph.

■ PRESENT TENSE AND PAST TENSE

• Use the present tense for describing actions that continue to happen regularly.

> Ms. Chu is responsible for our San Francisco region.
>
> Val Codresciu designs all our brochures.

• Use the simple past tense to tell your own stories or stories from history.

> The first time I tried Jello I was four years old.
>
> President Truman waved from the caboose.

■ TROUBLESOME VERBS

HAD

Watch out for *had:* You often don't need it. Use *had* to refer to events that were already finished when your story or example took place—the past before the past that you're describing. To check, try adding *previously* or *already* next to *had.*

> In 1986, the firm moved to New York. We had practiced in Florida for three years.
>
> If I had known about tse-tse flies, I would have been much more cautious.

WOULD

Most of the time, you can leave out *would.* Use it for something that happened regularly during a period of the past.

> In the early days of automobiles, tires would blow out routinely.

Also use *would* for hypothetical situations.

> I would have preferred that we hired Spencer.
>
> If we had hired Spencer, we would have that account in Japan right now.
>
> If Grayson were more responsible, we would never have lost that account.

(Use *were* with a singular subject after *if* or *as though*.)

COULD, CAN

- Use *could* to refer to the past and *can* to refer to the present.

  > *Past:*   The engineers couldn't run the experiment because the ocean was too rough.
  >
  > *Present:*   The engineers can't run the experiment because the ocean is too rough.

- Use *could* to show what might happen and doesn't; use *can* to show ability.

  > This company makes huge profits. They could provide free day care. (They don't.)
  >
  > This company makes such huge profits that they can provide free day care. (They do.)

47 WORD ENDINGS: *S* AND *ED*

If word endings give you problems, train yourself to check every noun to see if it needs *s* and every verb to see if it needs *s* or *ed*. Note that often these endings are barely pronounced.

ADD *ED*

- To form most simple past tenses

  She walked.   He tripped.   Mae asked a question.

- After *has, have, had*

  He has walked.   We have moved.   She had already arrived.

- After the *be* verbs (*are, were, is, was, am, be, been, being*)

  This manager was prejudiced against immigrants.

  That real estate market is depressed.

  Marge Zolanski is engaged to be married.

Note that the *-ed* ending can sometimes appear in present and future tenses:

  The gifts for premium customers are supposed to arrive on Friday.

  Following his speech, Mr. Poppins will be prepared to respond to reporters' questions.

DO NOT ADD *ED*

- After *to*

  Rosa Sanchez preferred to work with our most difficult cases.

- After *would, should, could*

  Sometimes she would work on weekends.

  This patient should walk for an hour every day.

- After *did, didn't*

  This software didn't save us any time.

- After an irregular past tense

    We bought the new system.

    The stock fell.

    The shoes cost only seventeen dollars.

ADD *S*

- To form a plural (more than one)

    many scientists   two potatoes

- To the present tense of a verb that follows *he, she, it,* or a singular noun

    He reports to the two vice presidents.

    She asks provocative questions.

    Polly insists on using the latest version.

    It costs very little.

    Note: Usually when there is an *s* on the noun, there is no *s* on the verb.

    Pots rattle.

    A pot rattles.

    The candles burn swiftly.

    The candle burns swiftly.

- To form a possessive (with an apostrophe)

    the director's requirements

    today's society

    Ms. Salama's office

    women's clothing

DO NOT ADD *S* TO A VERB

- If the subject of the sentence is plural or if there are two subjects

    Tulips come from Holland.

    Salt and sugar look the same.

- If one of these helping verbs comes before the main verb

does	may	will	shall	can
must	might	would	should	could

  Mr. Smoot can clear up all of your software conflicts.

  A heavy rainstorm might ruin this carefully planned reception.

  The new regulation does make me angry.

For more help with word endings, see Chapters 39, 45, 46, and 53 ("Spelling," "Verbs: Agreement with Subjects," "Verbs: Consistent Tenses," and "Apostrophes").

PART
SIX

CORRECTNESS:
PUNCTUATION

48 PERIODS: AVOIDING SENTENCE FRAGMENTS AND RUN-ON SENTENCES

Often you reach a pause in your writing, and you wonder, "Do I put a comma or a period?" The length of a sentence has nothing to do with the right choice. You need to look at what comes before and after the punctuation to see whether you have two separate sentences or a sentence plus a sentence fragment.

■ RECOGNIZING SENTENCE FRAGMENTS

WORDS THAT RARELY BEGIN SENTENCES

Certain words almost never begin sentences:

such as	when
especially	which
that	who ⎫
not	how ⎬ except in a question
like, just like	what ⎭
the same as	

These words extend the previous sentence. In most cases, put a comma or a dash before these words.

Incorrect: The attached report was translated from the Japanese original. Which was based on Monday morning's data.

Correct: The attached report was translated from the Japanese original, which was based on Monday morning's data.

Incorrect: Michael Kahn has edited all of Steven Spielberg's films over the last twenty years. Such as *Close Encounters of the Third Kind* and *Saving Private Ryan*.

Correct: Michael Kahn has edited all of Steven Spielberg's films over the last twenty years–such as *Close Encounters of the Third Kind* and *Saving Private Ryan.*

Incorrect: I believe that Whitman is our most successful salesperson. That he single-handedly built up American Pottery.

Correct: I believe that Whitman is our most successful salesperson, that he single-handedly built up American Pottery.

Note: *That* rarely begins a sentence, except when it points, as in "That was the year of the great flood."

SUBORDINATING WORDS

Certain words always begin half a sentence—either the first half or the second half. These are called subordinating words.

when	if
before	because
after	although (even though)
as	unless
while	since

A sentence fragment often begins with a subordinating word:

Incorrect: Even though I always fly business class.

You can fix this fragment by connecting it to the sentence before or after it:

Correct: I find air travel extremely stressful even though I always fly business class.

Correct: Even though I always fly business class, I find air travel extremely stressful.

You can also drop the subordinating word:

Correct: I find air travel extremely stressful.

A subtle point: Watch out for *and.* Putting *and* between a fragment and a sentence doesn't fix the fragment:

> *Still incorrect:* Even though I always fly business class and I find air travel extremely stressful.

VERBS IN AN INAPPROPRIATE FORM

Certain verb forms cannot be the only verb in the sentence.

Verbs Ending in -*ing*

> *Incorrect:* This film abounds with irreverent energy. Carrying the audience along with outrageous humor.

One solution is to connect the fragment to the previous sentence:

> *Correct:* This film abounds with irreverent energy, carrying the audience along with outrageous humor.

The second solution is to change the -*ing* verb to a complete verb:

> *Correct:* This film abounds with irreverent energy. It carries the audience along with outrageous humor.

An -*ing* verb can begin a sentence if a complete verb comes later:

> *Correct:* Keeping the audience in hysterics is Mel Brooks's trademark.

To Verbs (Infinitives)

To verbs also frequently begin fragments:

> *Incorrect:* Here's a voucher for two tickets to *The Lion King* with our compliments. To apologize for inconveniencing you this morning.

Fix these fragments by connecting them to the sentence before or by adding a subject and verb:

> *Correct:* Here's a voucher for two tickets to *The Lion King* with our compliments, to apologize for inconveniencing you this morning.

> *Correct:* Here's a voucher for two tickets to *The Lion King* with our compliments. We wish to apologize for inconveniencing you this morning.

REPEATED WORDS

A repeated word can begin a fragment:

> *Incorrect:* Elizabeth is the ideal supervisor. A supervisor who is both encouraging and demanding.

The best solution here is to replace the period with a comma.

> *Correct:* Elizabeth is the ideal supervisor, a supervisor who is both encouraging and demanding.

■ HOW TO FIX FRAGMENTS

- Attach the fragment to the previous sentence.

> *Incorrect:* Of course talking to your plants helps them grow. Because you're giving them a good dose of carbon dioxide.

> *Correct:* Of course talking to your plants helps them grow because you're giving them a good dose of carbon dioxide.

- Change the phrasing or omit the word that points to the previous sentence. Often this word will be a subordinating word.

> *Correct:* Of course talking to your plants helps them grow. You're giving them a good dose of carbon dioxide.

- Change the verb or add a verb (and, if necessary, a subject).

> *Incorrect:* I'm writing to commend Tony Zurlo to your attention. To provide further evidence of his considerable expertise.

> *Correct:* I'm writing to commend Tony Zurlo to your attention. I hope to provide further evidence of his considerable expertise.

USING FRAGMENTS FOR STYLE

Professional writers use sentence fragments for emphasis or style. Once you have control over the basics of sentence structure and punctuation, you can experiment. In the right spot, fragments can be strong. Very strong.

■ RECOGNIZING RUN-ON SENTENCES

A run-on sentence happens when you have two complete sentences, but you have only a comma or no punctuation between them. Run-ons usually occur because the two sentences are closely related. The two most common spots where run-ons occur are

- When a pronoun begins the second sentence:

  Incorrect: The news team has been stranded by the flood, they won't be able to deliver the tapes.

  Correct: The news team has been stranded by the flood. They won't be able to deliver the tapes.

  Incorrect: This lemon zester is ergonometrically designed, it's comfortable to use.

  Correct: This lemon zester is ergonometrically designed; it's comfortable to use.

- When *however* begins the second sentence:

  Incorrect: We can control the noise level in all the cubicles, however we will have to charge an additional fee.

  Correct: We can control the noise level in all the cubicles. However, we will have to charge an additional fee.

■ HOW TO FIX RUN-ON SENTENCES

  Run-on: My cleaning staff will keep your home ready for company, we're both thorough and fast.

- Insert a period between the two sentences.

    Correct: My cleaning staff will keep your home ready for company. We're both thorough and fast.

- Insert a semicolon between the two sentences.

    Correct: My cleaning staff will keep your home ready for company; we're both thorough and fast.

- Insert a comma and a coordinating conjunction between the two sentences.

    Correct: My cleaning staff will keep your home ready for company, for we're both thorough and fast.

- Insert a subordinating word before one of the sentences.

    Correct: My cleaning staff will keep your home ready for company because we're both thorough and fast.

49 COMMAS

These days, more errors come from having too many commas than from having too few.

Writing trends, especially in business writing, have moved more and more into "open" punctuation—that is, punctuation which de-emphasizes the use of commas when a sentence can be clearly read without them. However, many businesses still adhere to "closed" punctuation—strict adherence to formal grammatical rules. When you elect to omit a comma, be certain that you are doing so as a choice, rather than as neglect.

Here are four places where commas are necessary.

■ COMMA BEFORE *BUT, AND, SO, YET, OR, FOR,* AND *NOR*

Put a comma before *but, and, so, yet, or, for,* and *nor* when they connect two sentences.

> The lead actor hobbled in on crutches, but the show went on.
>
> Rosette plays a hard game of tennis three times a week, and she intends to enter the county tournament next spring.
>
> Not only will a deskside paper shredder keep your desktop clear, but it will also ensure privacy of information.
>
> The agent took too long to respond, so we have withdrawn the offer.

However, don't automatically stick in a comma just because a sentence is long.

> Conferees are invited to meet in the lobby at 6:45 for refreshments prior to the convocation at 7:30 P.M.

■ COMMAS IN A LIST OR SERIES

Use commas between parts of a series of three or more.

In less than one month the game farm has saved the lives of a red fox, a great horned owl, a mountain lion, and a black bear cub.

The auctioneer moved through the 100 items rapidly, sold all but 4 of them, and kept the audience laughing the whole time.

Refinement The final comma in a series (which usually precedes *and*) is sometimes omitted when not essential to the sense of the sentence.

The auctioneer moved through the 100 items rapidly, sold all but 4 of them and kept the audience laughing the whole time.

I wanted to buy toothpaste, jumper cables, a potted plant, cookies and fabric all in one store.

Take care, however, when omitting the final comma: be certain you don't need it for clarity.

In the waiting room sat a bearded man, a police officer, a woman eating a sandwich, and a parakeet in a cage.

(Without the last comma, what happens to the parakeet?)

Don't use a comma in a pair.

Rosette plays a hard game of tennis three times a week and intends to enter the county tournament next spring.

In one month the game farm saved the lives of a red fox and a great horned owl.

Sue and Brian volunteered to prepare the agenda and get the report to the subcommittee by Wednesday.

■ Comma After a Lead-in

Use a comma after an introductory part of a sentence.

However, Ms. Capone has improved her presentation skills dramatically.

For example, state law requires an inventory of properties before the will can be probated.

Arthur, will you please keep notes on the meeting proceedings?

After lunch, there will be a hands-on workshop in C319.

During the entire four hours of the hearing, the district attorney never even sat down.

When the Tokyo market closes on Friday, we will make another evaluation.

Refinement The comma is often omitted after a very short introductory word or phrase when you do not need or want a voice pause. Words such as *nevertheless, however,* and *therefore* generally take a comma because they require a voice pause. In the following examples, either sentence is considered correct.

After lunch, there will be a hands-on workshop in C319.
After lunch there will be a hands-on workshop in C319.

In time, we will all know exactly what happened.
In time we will all know exactly what happened.

■ A PAIR OF COMMAS AROUND AN INSERTION

Surround an insertion or interruption with a pair of commas. Both commas are necessary, since a single comma would separate the subject from its verb.

The truth, however, finally came out.

Woody Guthrie, the father of Arlo Guthrie, wrote "This Land Is Your Land."

The office manager, Jennie Pocock, who leaves after twenty-two years of incomparable service, will be difficult to replace.

Judith Appelbaum, in her book *How to Get Happily Published,* gives numerous suggestions for working with a publisher or for going the self-publishing route.

Places and dates are treated as insertions. Note especially that commas surround the year and the state.

Honesdale, Pennsylvania, was named for Philip Hone, former mayor of New York and president of the coal company.

I was born on August 15, 1954, at seven in the morning.

Filming will begin in Sullivan Bay, British Columbia, March or April, 2000, depending on Ms. Wright's availability.

Refinement Commas are not used when the interruption is essential to the meaning of the sentence—that is, when the word or phrase could not be omitted.

The scanner on the third floor is best for your project.
(There are other scanners—on different floors.)

50 SEMICOLONS AND COLONS

■ SEMICOLONS

Semicolons can be used instead of periods; they also can separate parts of a complicated list.

Use a semicolon to connect two related sentences; each half must be a complete sentence.

> This company was in crisis two years ago; Jane Morgan's quiet professionalism made the transition to solvency possible.

> It's not that O'Hara's position is wrong; it's that he misses the key point.

A semicolon often comes before certain transition words; a comma follows the transition.

however	therefore	otherwise
nevertheless	in other words	instead
for example	on the other hand	meanwhile
besides	furthermore	fortunately

> Our competitors offer some important benefits; however, we offer those same benefits plus more, at a lower cost.

> The bank lost two of my deposits; therefore, I am closing my account.

Semicolons work best when used to emphasize a strong connection between the two sentences.

Use semicolons, instead of commas, in a list when some of the parts already have commas.

> To make it as an actor, you need, first of all, some natural talent; second, the habits of discipline and concentration; and third, the ability to promote yourself.

■ COLONS

Colons create suspense: they can set up a list, a quotation, or an emphatic statement.

Use a colon after a complete sentence to introduce related details.

Before a colon you must have a complete statement. Don't use a colon after *are* or *include* or *such as*.

Colons can introduce

- A list

    In addition to bringing their personal supplies, clients are responsible for providing these items: a sleeping bag, a water bottle, and a backpack.

- A quotation

    The author begins with a shocker: "Mother spent her summer sitting naked on a rock."

- An example

    Increase your use of legumes: for example, beans or lentils.

- An emphatic assertion

    This is the bottom line: Meredith refuses the contract without a guarantee of protection for her heirs.

- A subtitle

    Rules of Thumb: A Guide for Writers

51 DASHES AND PARENTHESES

In general, dashes highlight or emphasize material whereas parentheses de-emphasize the material within them.

■ DASHES

Dashes highlight the part of the sentence they separate, or show an abrupt change of thought in midsentence, or connect a fragment to a sentence.

> Artemesia–which craves dry heat–is the perfect border plant for rock gardens in the Southwest.

> Cell-phone conversations–or e-mail messages, for that matter–should not be considered private.

> Johnson and Ryman will offer a substantial collection of Fiestaware–a collection remarkable for its pristine condition and variety of colors.

Dashes can replace a period, comma, colon, or semicolon. However—handy though they are—too many can make it seem as if you've dashed off your report.

When you type, two hyphens make a dash; there is no space before or after the dash.

■ PARENTHESES

Parentheses de-emphasize the words they separate. Use them to enclose brief explanations or interruptions. They can contain either part of a sentence or a whole sentence.

> We offered at the regional average price per acre ($995) and settled at $800.

> Ms. Hasie has had two extremely successful years in sales. (See the attached reports.)

> This proposal has plagued the creative team (three designers have worked on it without resolution); so at this point, I recommend that we decline the commission.

- Put any necessary punctuation after the second parenthesis if the parentheses contain part of a sentence.

- If the parentheses contain a complete sentence, put the period inside the second parenthesis. Notice, however, that you don't capitalize or use a period when parentheses enclose a sentence within a sentence.

Be sparing with parentheses. Too many can chop up your sentences.

52 HYPHENS

Hyphens join compound words.

> self-employed
> in-laws
> seventy-five
> happy-go-lucky

Hyphens are currently enjoying a comeback, thanks to the Internet and the new electronic world.

> e-mail   e-text   e-commerce   e-filing

- Hyphens make a two-word adjective before a noun, but not after it.

  > Gary Larson is a well-known cartoonist.
  > Gary Larson is well known as a cartoonist.

  > Balloons, as a means of flying, were a late eighteenth-century invention.

  > Balloons were a means of flying in the late eighteenth century.

- Note that there is no space before or after a hyphen.

53 APOSTROPHES

Most of the time, when you add an *s* to a word you don't need an apostrophe. Use apostrophes for contractions and possessives.

Do not add an apostrophe; just add *s* or *es*.

- To make a plural

    Two bosses   Three CDs   500 free passes

- To a present-tense verb

    He sees.   She says.   It talks.   Carol sings.

Add an apostrophe.

- To a contraction (the apostrophe replaces the missing letter).

doesn't = does not	it's = it is	that's = that is
don't	I'm	weren't
didn't	you're	what's

- To a possessive.

the company's policy	a director's style	a good night's sleep
Gus's hair	children's toys	a family's history
Ms. Jones's opinion	women's room	today's world

- If the word is plural and already ends with *s,* add an apostrophe after the *s.*

    my accounts' total value (several accounts)
    grandparents' beliefs

- Pronouns in possessive form have no apostrophe.

    its   hers   his   ours   theirs   yours

- Use an apostrophe for the plural of letters used as letters.

    In this typeface, *q*'s and *g*'s are too similar.

54 QUOTATION MARKS

Use quotation marks for someone else's exact words, or for words or phrases that you discuss out of context.

Quotations in this chapter come from the following selection of *Robert's Rules of Order* by Henry M. Robert (1915):

> The object of *Rules of Order* is to assist an assembly to accomplish in the best possible manner the work for which it was designed. To do this it is necessary to restrain the individual somewhat, as the right of an individual, in any community, to do what he pleases, is incompatible with the interests of the whole. Where there is no law, but every man does what is right in his own eyes, there is the least of real liberty.

■ PUNCTUATION BEFORE A QUOTATION

Here are three ways to lead into a quotation:

- For short quotations (a word or a phrase), don't use *"Robert's Rules of Order* says," and don't put a comma before the quotation. Simply use the writer's phrase as it fits smoothly into your sentence:

  > Robert finds it essential to "restrain the individual somewhat" for the sake of orderly discussion.

- Put a comma before the quotation marks if you use "he says." Put no comma if you use "he says that."

  > Robert says, "Where there is no law, but every man does what is right in his own eyes, there is the least of real liberty."

  > Robert says that "it is necessary to restrain the individual somewhat."

- Use a colon (:) before a quotation of a sentence or more. Be sure you have a complete statement before the colon. Don't use "he says."

In one sentence, Robert pulls together the philosophy behind his book: "Where there is no law, but every man does what is right in his own eyes, there is the least of real liberty."

■ Punctuation After a Quotation

At the end of a quotation, the period or comma goes inside the quotation marks. Do not close the quotation marks as you move from one sentence to the next until the person's words end. Use one mark of punctuation to end your sentence—never two periods or a comma and a period.

Semicolons go outside of closing quotation marks.

Robert says, "It is necessary to restrain the individual somewhat"; nevertheless, he does so in the interest of "real liberty."

Question marks and exclamation marks go inside if the person quoted is asking or exclaiming. (If you are asking or exclaiming, the mark goes outside.)

"Have you mastered the ins and outs of *Robert's Rules of Order*?" the delegate asked.

What does Robert mean by "real liberty"?

■ Indenting Long Quotations

Long quotations (more than three lines) do not get quotation marks. Instead, start on a new line and indent the whole left margin of the quotation. After the quotation, return to the original margin and continue your paragraph.

Henry Robert had thoughtfully considered the implications of his work:

To do this [conduct an effective meeting] it is necessary to restrain the individual somewhat [...]. Where there is no law, but every man does what is right in his own eyes, there is the least of real liberty.

Use brackets ([ ]) around a changed word or added explanation.

Use an ellipsis (three periods, with a space before and after each), in brackets, to indicate an omission.

Use sic—"as it stood"—in brackets to indicate an error in the original.

> Jamiesen writes: "The principle [sic] effect is chaos."

■ DIALOGUE

In dialogue, start a new paragraph every time you switch from one speaker to the other.

> A lively exchange ended the meeting:
>
> "I totally reject your conclusions! I am not convinced that this research is without bias!" S.B. shouted.
>
> "Not without the bias of your assumptions, you mean!" growled P.H.
>
> "This meeting is adjourned!" ruled the chair.

■ WRITING ABOUT A WORD OR PHRASE

When you discuss a word or phrase, surround it with quotation marks.

> Advertisers use "America," while news reporters refer to "the United States."

Do not use quotation marks around slang; either use the word without quotation marks or find a better word.

■ QUOTATION WITHIN A QUOTATION

For quotations within a quotation, use single quotation marks:

> According to radio announcer Rhingo Lake, "The jockey clearly screamed 'I've been foiled!' as the horse fell to the ground right before the finish line."

■ QUOTING POETRY

For poetry, when quoting two or more lines, indent from the left margin and copy the lines of poetry exactly as the poet arranged them.

> We are such stuff
> As dreams are made on; and our little life
> Is rounded with a sleep.

When quoting a few words of poetry that include a line break, use a slash mark to show where the poet's line ends.

> In *The Tempest*, Shakespeare calls us "such stuff / As dreams are made on. . . ."

When a line of poetry is too long to fit on a line of your paper, indent the turnover line an additional three spaces, as in the following line from Walt Whitman's *Leaves of Grass.*

> I believe that a leaf of grass is no less than the journeywork
>   of the stars.

55 Italicizing (Underlining) or Quoting Titles

Italicize or underline titles of longer works; use quotation marks for titles of shorter works that are published within the longer works.

- *Italicize* or <u>underline</u> titles of longer works, such as books, magazines, plays, newspapers, movies, and television programs.

  Saturday Night Live   *War and Peace*
  The Wall Street Journal   *The Wizard of Oz*

  Don't mix underlining and italics for titles in the same document. In e-mail, use the underline before and after the title.

  The Art of Kissing, Tickling, and Being Bored.

- Put "quotation marks" around titles of shorter works, such as articles, chapter titles, poems, songs, and short stories.

  "U.S. on Track for Surplus"   "The Star-Spangled Banner"

  Remember that a comma or period, if needed, goes inside the quotation marks.

  In "Talk, Type, Read E-Mail," Amy Harmon discusses the intricacies of juggling several tasks on the computer.

- Journalists use quotation marks for all titles; use that format for press releases and articles you submit to nonscholarly publications.

- Do not italicize or place quotation marks around your title on a cover sheet—unless your title contains someone else's title:

  Analysis of Salamander Population in Oxbow Tributary 1992–99

  Proposed Modifications to *Murder in the Tanning Salon*, Scene 7

  Capitalize only the first word and all major words in a title.

APPENDIX

Sample Memo
Sample Bad News Memo
Sample Letter
Sample Letter of Recommendation
Sample Meeting Agenda
Two Sample Press Releases
Sample Cover Letter
Sample Résumé (Emphasis on Accomplishments)
Sample Résumé (Emphasis on Skills)
Sample Résumé (Limited Experience)
Sample Résumé (Significant Experience)
The Anatomy of a Sentence: How to Diagram
A List of Important References

SAMPLE MEMO

Bromelain
Research
Group   One Highview Drive,
Indianapolis, IN 46222

Date: June 10, 1999
To: All Employees
From: Deana Bartlett 𝒟𝓑   dbartlett@Bromelain.com
Executive Vice President   Phone   317.636.1500
Fax   317.636.1560
Re: Employee Stock Option Purchase Plan

To encourage stock ownership by employees of the Bromelain Research Group and its subsidiaries, the board of directors has adopted a new Employee Stock Option Purchase Plan (ESOPP). We expect stockholder approval of this plan by July 1, 1999, and that the Plan will become active by September 1, 1999.

The principal provision of ESOPP will be to offer all employees who work at least twenty hours per week an opportunity to purchase company stock through payroll deductions. The price at which the employee may purchase the stock is 85 percent of the last reported sale price of the BRG common stock on the day the offering period ends.

An employee may elect to have up to 10 percent of his or her salary deducted for the purpose of purchasing stock. In no event may an employee's total deduction or payment during a calendar year exceed $5000.

No person will be eligible to participate in ESOPP if he or she would be treated for tax purposes as possessing 5 percent or more of the voting power or value of BRG's common stock. The BRG Board of Directors retains the right to determine ineligibility of any employee, particularly those employees who are considered "highly compensated" by the company.

As of June 1, 1999, approximately 1730 persons were eligible to participate in ESOPP.

ESOPP will be administered by the Management Development and Compensation Committee, which is authorized to make rules and regulations for the administration and interpretation of the plans.

SAMPLE BAD NEWS MEMO

> **DELLMORE CORPORATION**
> 45678 Peachtree Avenue
> Atlanta, GA 30318

Date: January 8, 1999

To: Pramila Varda
Director, Interface Dept.

From: Jason C. Whitmore   jcwhitmore@Dellmore.com
Vice President for Human Resources   Phone   404-355-2496
Fax   404-355-2497

Subject: Confirmation of Future Staffing Revisions

This memorandum specifies your department's staff reductions resulting from our recent merger with ISF.

As described during the December 4 meeting, the DellMore Corporation Executive Committee hopes to ensure the least disruptive adjustment to our recent merger. We are counting on you and the other directors to ease any problems resulting from the reduction of existing staff.

The merger requires the integration of our two interface departments. This consolidation will reduce DellMore's interface staff from twelve to seven individuals:

—Transfer or termination of two supervisors
—Transfer or termination of two level 2 clerks
—Transfer or termination of one secretary

We are very well aware of the difficulty of a transition like this. Every effort will be made to accommodate individual needs and to relocate staff within the new ISF corporation. In the next few weeks, Paul Mooney will be meeting with you to help you evaluate Interface Department staff. Meanwhile, please feel free to call Paul if you have particular questions or concerns.

We very much regret the hardship this reduction will entail. However, a reinvigorated DellMore within ISF will ultimately bring the greatest benefit to the greatest number of our employees.

cc: Paul Mooney, Director of Human Resources

SAMPLE LETTER

One Education Drive
Garden City, NY 11530-6793

ENGLISH DEPARTMENT   516-572-7185

31 October 1997

Ms. Kiera Cunningham
Designer
McGraw-Hill Higher Education Group
1333 Burr Ridge Pkwy.
Burr Ridge, IL 60521

Re: Silverman, Hughes, & Wienbroer. *Rules of Thumb 4/e*

Dear Kiera:

As I told you on the phone, this is the cleanest, most attractive set of page designs we've ever seen, and we are particularly grateful for your detailed response to the number of design concerns we submitted with the manuscript. Many thanks for your care and creativity.

You have responded to nearly all of our issues. We have just a few remaining requests.

White space

We would like more vertical space above subheadings—proportionate to the level of the head, rather than identical space above heads regardless of level—as currently spaced on page 10 of the layout sheets. We would also like a little more space below each subheading—more than you have, but the same regardless of level of head—not proportionate.

Titles and Headings

We particularly like the elegance and lightness of the section titles and the variety of typefaces for subheadings. As you write the specs, will you include a reminder that we don't automatically follow the hierarchy of heads as if it were an outline? Sometimes we prefer a bulleted list in a major section.

Graphics

Perhaps we could have smaller bullets—even dots? In general, we prefer bullets to tildes, but where we need subdivisions under bullets (only in a couple of places in the book), we prefer the tilde rather than the hyphen.

We realize that these are a number of requests. For our part, we promise speedy responses at later stages to facilitate the production schedule.

Please call me at the college if you have any questions.

Thanks again for all your help.

Diana

Diana Roberts Wienbroer—also for Jay Silverman and Elaine Hughes

cc: Tim Julet, English Editor, McGraw-Hill

SAMPLE LETTER OF RECOMMENDATION

Holly Sherman Pena ■ **Charter Systems Inc.** ■ **Austin, TX 78766**

April 18, 1999

Mr. Anthony Varricchio
Lincoln County Office Systems
P O Box 339
Diamondville, Wyoming 83116

Re: Mildred Tarns, Applicant for Office Manager

Dear Mr. Varricchio:

I am writing to recommend an exceptional candidate for your consideration. Mildred Tarns would make a substantial contribution to your organization should you select her to be your office manager.

   I have supervised Mildred in her position as office manager at Charter Systems for the last seven years. Ours is a small firm specializing in installation of office systems—three partners and six temporary technical assistants. We also hire additional consultants on an as-needed basis. Mildred's job is to coordinate and provide transition as the various part-timers submit reports, claims, and referrals to our company. Over the years, we have all benefited from Mildred's organizational strategies and attention to detail.

   Mildred is supremely qualified for the position of office manager at your company. She is both businesslike and friendly.

■ The first thing that you will notice about Mildred is her energy and enthusiasm. Mildred pays attention to people, is genuinely interested in their problems, and remembers them. This is a major asset to the front office of any organization.

■ Mildred is an organizer, with an intuitive understanding of the simplest solution. She'll have everything in efficient order in record time.

■ Mildred is a producer. She will take a task (the company picnic, for example) and make it happen in a truly professional, fun way.

■ On a personal note, Mildred has strong values. She respects those around her; she is consistent in her expectations of her own performance (and unflinching when wrongs need to be addressed, for example at a public forum); and she practices the golden rule.

   Please feel free to call or write if you wish further information from me. I write in support of what will surely be a loss to us, but Mildred and her husband are determined to move to your area, so I hope that you will welcome them.

Very truly yours,

Holly Pena

Holly Sherman Pena
Vice President, Charter Systems

hspena@chartersys.com ■ **Phone 512.572.6676** ■ **Fax 512.572.6677**

SAMPLE MEETING AGENDA

JDE AND ASSOCIATES / 1739 Ambar Drive / Calabasas, CA 91360

Interdepartmental Memo

Date: July 12, 1999

To: Jack Adams, Amy Fong, Woody Rainey, Juanita Valdez, and Ben Zapolski

From: Sheila Thomes 〤   818-340-6666
Director, Studio B   SThomes@JDEassoc.com

Subject: Final Meeting on Proposal for Sheffield Gardens
Thursday, July 15, 1999, 10:00 a.m. PDT Conference Room 4

AGENDA

1. Approval of Minutes July 8, 1999, attached
2. Report from Juanita on revised test results
3. Report from Jack on section 16: bar graphs
4. Report from Sheila on printing and packaging
5. Approval of press release, attached
6. Discussion of final issues
   - Delivery of documents
   - Follow-through with Mr. Dolan

Please be prompt. I've arranged for coffee/tea at 10 and for lunch to be brought in at 12:30. Let's try to adjourn by 5 P.M.

SAMPLE PRESS RELEASE

PRESS RELEASE for distribution 11:00 A.M. MST, November 6, 1999

Selkirk Labs, Inc.
Six Research Blvd.
Boulder, CO. 88999

SELKIRK LABS TO ACQUIRE ARGO TECHNOLOGY

Selkirk Labs, a leading manufacturer of computer parts, agreed today to buy Argo Technology for $9.5 million in cash, thus beginning an expansion into the software business.

Under this agreement, made through Selkirk's SLI investment unit, Selkirk is to pay 32 percent more than the Friday closing price of Argo.

Argo Technology, a small software company based in Palo Alto, California, scored its first major market hit last year with its best-selling *Aware!,* a program designed to gather news from a wide variety of sources using each client's interests and preferences.

Cara Copland, spokesperson for Selkirk Labs, says this purchase "provides a major channel for our new commitment to service." The purchase represents the first acquisition in a program of planned expansion undertaken by Selkirk last year.

Argo will continue to operate as a separate subsidiary of Selkirk Labs but will move its offices to Boulder where Selkirk is located.

Negotiations are already underway for purchase of suitable property for Argo's new facility, now in final designing stages. Copland says Selkirk anticipates that the acquisition should be completed during the first quarter of 2000.

SELKIRK CONTACT: Bess Lanier
303.777.9077
Fax 303.777.9088
b_lanier@selkirk.com

ARGO CONTACT: Fred Elsasser
916.362.7033
Fax 916.384.3084
Felsass@ARGO.com

SAMPLE PRESS RELEASE

PRESS RELEASE
for distribution 6:00 P.M. MDT, July 23, 1999

Sunstripe Corporation
10632 Colorado Street
Santa Fe, NM 87504

Contact: Greg Samler
505.342.4429
Fax 505.777.9088
gsamler@sunstripe.com

SUNSTRIPE CORPORATION TO DONATE RECREATION SITE

Sunstripe Corporation, the largest U.S. manufacturer of portable canvas resort tents, has announced plans to convert 10 acres of their 200-acre surroundings into a small beach and recreation site which will be open to the public.

Jodie Archer, Vice President for Customer Relations, calls the new project "a return gift to the Santa Fe community. We've enjoyed nine years of unprecedented growth since moving our plant here from Pittsburgh. This is our way of saying 'thank you' to the residents of this area."

Sunstripe tents are used by resorts all over the world. In keeping with the theme of their product, Sunstripe plans to create a machine-made sandy beach with playground and picnic areas around Lake Dunsworth. Sunstripe promises maintenance and staffing of the area, with facilities for swimming, rowing, and fishing.

Plans are still in the early stage, but Ms. Archer expects to have further details and a sketch of the planned site available to the public by the end of November. Sunstripe has targeted February as the groundbreaking and hopes to have the recreation area open to the public by midsummer of next year.

Sunstripe's grounds are located 16 miles east of downtown Santa Fe and can be easily reached via major thoroughfares.

SAMPLE COVER LETTER FOR RÉSUMÉ

Joylene A. Bigelow
1805 Eisenhower Drive
Clinton, MS 39056
601-924-2892

June 16, 1999

Ms. Betty Taylor
Vice President for Human Resources
Kirtley Pharmaceuticals
3905 Chickasaw Dr.
Jackson, MS 39216

Dear Ms. Taylor:

Jay Berman told me that Kirtley Pharmaceuticals plans to reorganize their training and development department and that you will soon be advertising for the new position of Director of Training.

As my résumé demonstrates, I have had a wide range of experience with staff development in the health care industry. In particular, my recent experience at Omni-Group Health Plans has fully prepared me for the position you are creating. You will also find that my knowledge of the nursing home and insurance businesses can be an asset to Kirtley's sales agents, as will my personal knowledge of potential clients.

I began my professional career as a nurse, but I have found true fulfillment as a teacher/coach. My approach emphasizes how employees promote the public image of the organization—through being better informed, more caring, and more thorough than the competition. I know that concern about Kirtley's image has prompted your decision to reorganize, and I would appreciate the chance to help.

Should you be interested in discussing my ideas, I would be happy to meet with you at your earliest convenience.

Yours truly,

Joylene A Bigelow

Joylene A. Bigelow

SAMPLE RÉSUMÉ
(EMPHASIS ON ACCOMPLISHMENTS)

Joylene A. Bigelow
1805 Eisenhower Drive
Clinton, MS 39056
601-924-2892

Objective: A management position in the Health Care Industry

Experience

Dec. 1993–   Omni-Group Health Plans, Inc.
June 1999   Director, Human Resources, Southern District Office

Hired, supervised, evaluated, scheduled, and managed a staff of 175–200
claims adjustors, accountants, and review panelists for the Claims
Division of this regional office of a national comprehensive health
insurance company. I also provided initial and ongoing training/education
for the staff. In 1995, I developed policies and procedures for streamlining
our response to clients' contested claims.

June 1992–   Director of Nursing
Nov. 1993   Vicksburg Trace Haven

Trace Haven is a 120-bed nursing facility with a 22-bed SNF. I was
responsible for interviewing, hiring, firing, supervising, and scheduling a
staff of over seventy employees. Attended therapy meetings, developed
forms and protocols, provided training, reviewed potential residents,
oversaw implementation of state regulations governing nursing facilities.

April 1991–   Staff Nurse
May 1992   ParkView Home Health

Conducted skilled nursing visits and completed required documentation
of care. Successfully introduced a system whereby each nurse's
assignment was made according to his/her caseload—and not randomly
as it had been in the past.

SAMPLE RÉSUMÉ (CONTINUED)

Joylene A. Bigelow page 2

Education
Bilingual (English-Spanish)

1973   Diploma in Nursing

Graduated with honors from a three-year diploma program at Mercy Hospital–Street Memorial School of Nursing, Vicksburg, and passed the State Board for Examination of Nurses with commendation.

1973–1978   In-Service Trainings

During these years, I worked in a variety of jobs in hospitals, research, comprehensive health center, and the Mississippi State Hospital at Whitfield. I participated in numerous job-specific classes covering such topics as wound care, hypertension, diabetes, management of people, interpersonal skills, nursing documentation, supervising difficult employees, time management, etc.

Note: From 1978–1988, I took time out from my profession to marry and raise two children. However, during those years I continued to develop skills relevant to my professional responsibilities.

Additional Accomplishments

1986–93   Chair of the Visitation Committee, All Angels Church

Responsible for coordinating parishioners' visits to the ill, infirm, and bereaved. I developed a network of volunteers who communicate via a simple phone chain to supplement the visits by the clergy.

1984–88   Coordinator for Welcome Wagon Services for the
                 Vicksburg area

Duties included training volunteer greeters, soliciting donations from area merchants, and computerizing the system for registry of new area residents.

1979–85   Volunteer Fundraiser, Annual Red Cross Fund Drive

Each year, for approximately six weeks, I recruited and trained volunteers to solicit donations. My team surpassed its funding goal each time.

SAMPLE RÉSUMÉ (EMPHASIS ON SKILLS)

Joylene A. Bigelow
1805 Eisenhower Drive
Clinton, MS 39056
601-924-2892

Objective: A management position in Human Resources

Qualifications

Management Skills

• Interviewed, hired, supervised, scheduled, and terminated staff in health care organizations with up to 200 employees
• Developed policies and procedures, forms, and protocols
• Oversaw implementation of state regulations governing nursing facilities

Training Skills

• Provided initial and ongoing training/education for staff at insurance company and nursing home
• Recruited and trained volunteers for Welcome Wagon and Red Cross

Organizational Skills

• Developed a system for equalizing nursing assignments in a high-quality home nursing organization
• Coordinated and developed a system to enable volunteers to visit church members in need

Education

1973   Honors Diploma in Nursing
            Mercy Hospital–Street
            Memorial School of Nursing,
            Vicksburg, MS

Certification, State Board for Examination of Nurses with commendation

Bilingual (English-Spanish)

SAMPLE RÉSUMÉ (CONTINUED)

Joylene A. Bigelow page 2

Work History

Dec. 1993– June 1999	Omni-Group Health Plans, Inc. Director, Human Resources, Southern District
June 1992– Nov. 1993	Director of Nursing Vicksburg Trace Haven Nursing Home
1986–93	Chair of the Visitation Committee All Angels Church, Vicksburg
April 1991– May 1992	Staff Nurse ParkView Home Health
1984–88	Coordinator, Welcome Wagon Services Vicksburg and environs
1979–85	Volunteer Fundraiser Annual Red Cross Fund Drive
1973–1978	A variety of jobs in hospitals, research, comprehensive health center, and the Mississippi State Hospital at Whitfield

SAMPLE RÉSUMÉ
(LIMITED EXPERIENCE)

Michael J. Waite
589 Brookview Road
St. Louis Missouri 65790
voice mail 408.999.3453   e-mail waitemj@aol.com

Objective: to design information technology that really works
in the workplace

Employment

June 1994–present
(firm supplying the St. Louis area with personalized installation and
service for intranets)

On-site programmer and trouble-shooter. Modified, installed, and
maintained personalized software for clients—many in high-data
industries with systems of over 100 workstations. Acquired skills
in solving problems quickly as well as meeting a variety of
business client needs.

1990–1993 (summers only)
Radio Shack, St. Louis, MO

Sales associate. Also assisted in electronic repairs. Acquired skills
in dealing with customers and in solving simple mechanical
problems.

Education

1988–94 University of Vermont B.S. in Computer Technology

Dean's list. Volunteer 1990–93 (three hours weekly, twelve weeks
per semester, seven semesters) training senior citizens in
computer use.

Also provided maintenance to computer systems in local public
schools.

1984–88 Washington High School, St. Louis, MO

Academic diploma. Odyssey of the Mind [intellectual teamwork
competitions], three years; state finalist 1987. Senior Master
Project: created an interactive computer game, "MouseHole."
Baseball Varsity, three years.

References and program samples available upon request.

SAMPLE RÉSUMÉ (SIGNIFICANT EXPERIENCE)

Carolyn Dunn
80 Crozier Road
Kent, Connecticut 06934
860-378-3242   c3866@aol.com

1999–present	Freelance Television Producer
1991–1999	Bozell Advertising Worldwide, Inc. New York, NY Vice President Executive Producer
1986–1991	Saatchi & Saatchi Worldwide, Inc. New York, NY Executive Vice President Director, Broadcast Operations
1982–86	DDB Needham Worldwide, Inc. New York, NY Senior Vice President Director, Broadcast Production
1978–82	Needham Worldwide, Inc. Los Angeles, CA Senior Vice President Director, Broadcast Production
1974–78	Steppingstone Productions, Inc. New York, NY Executive Producer President and Owner

Manhattanville College
Purchase, NY
B.A. Degree

ANATOMY OF A SENTENCE: HOW TO DIAGRAM

Try diagramming a troublesome sentence to figure out what modifies what.

When you can't fix a problem sentence, analyzing how the parts connect can help you see where the trouble is. You can map out (diagram) the structure of your sentence. When you find a place for all the parts as you have written them, you can discover

- the parts that need to be rearranged

- the parts that need to be rephrased

- the parts (perhaps even whole sentences) that should be separated or dropped

Here are the basic techniques for diagramming, followed by several diagrammed sentences.

HOW TO DIAGRAM

- Write the subject, verb, and object (or complement) on a horizontal line.

- Draw a vertical line (through the horizontal line) to divide the subject and verb.

- Draw a short vertical line (which stops at the horizontal line) before the direct object.

- Draw a line leaning back to the subject before the complement.

- Write modifiers on horizontal lines under the word they modify.

- Separate the preposition from its object with a short vertical line.

- Use horizontal parallel lines for parallel parts—plural subjects, verbs, clauses, and so on.

- Use a horizontal line raised on a carat (^) for phrases or clauses that *as a unit* serve as subject or object.

Samples of Diagramming

Marlon deserves a promotion.

Marlon is the subject; *deserves* is the verb; *promotion* is the direct object; *a* modifies *promotion*.

This disk is full.

Disk is the subject; *is* is the verb; *full* is the complement; *this* modifies disk.

We will close early on Tuesday.

We is the subject; *will close* is the verb; *early* and the prepositional phrase *on Tuesday* modify *will close*.

Turkeys and white-tailed deer roam freely in Lebanon Township.

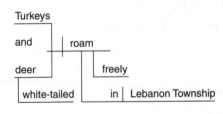

Turkeys and *deer* are the subjects; *and* is the conjunction that joins them; *white-tailed* modifies *deer*; *roam* is the verb; *freely* modifies *roam*; the prepositional phrase *in Lebanon Township* also modifies *roam*.

Samples of Diagramming (Continued)

Our goal is to serve the tastiest salads in the city.

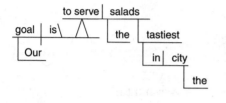

Goal is the subject; *is* is the verb; the complement that modifies the subject *goal* is an infinitive phrase—*to serve the tastiest salads in the city. To serve* is the infinitive; *salads* is its object; *the* and *tastiest* modify *salads.*

If you accept the new rental space, we will pay for all moving expenses.

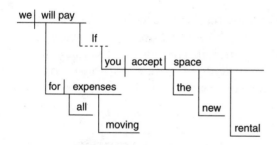

In the main sentence, *we* is the subject; *will pay* is the verb; *for expenses* modifies the verb, and *all* and *moving* modify *expenses.* Subordinated to the main sentence is the first sentence, connected by *if.* In the subordinated sentence, *you* is the subject; *accept* is the verb, and *the, new,* and *rental* modify *space.*

A LIST OF IMPORTANT REFERENCES

Internet addresses listed here are regularly updated on McGraw-Hill's website:

> http://www.mhhe.com/writers

Every day, more resources are available online. Your local library may offer software and passwords so you can access major databases free from your home or office; your business organization may provide additional access. However, even when a fee is required at a particular site, often it applies only to the ordering of a specific document. You may be able to get what you need by logging on and checking the free pages.

Your writing needs may require you to visit a library, subscribe regularly to professional journals, and/or buy key reference books and CD-ROMs. Check this list for some suggestions.

The following list does not separate resources according to format (print, CD-ROM, Internet) because the publication of material is gradually changing from print to digital. There is an advantage to each version; you may prefer to download and print information from a CD-ROM or the Internet, work with it, and then return to the computer.

HELP WITH CREATIVITY AND WRITER'S BLOCK

Hughes, Elaine Farris. *Writing from the Inner Self.* New York: HarperCollins, 1991. Offers techniques and advice to free your creative, real self. This book is particularly helpful if you have to produce fresh, innovative material regularly.

HELP WITH STYLE, GRAMMAR, AND USAGE

Booher, Dianna. *Good Grief, Good Grammar: A Business Person's Guide to Grammar and Usage.* New York: Ballantine, 1988. An easy-to-use, detailed guide to grammatical terms and their applications—for example, when to use *since* rather than *because.*

Jack Lynch's page—*Grammar and Style Notes*
⟨http://andromeda.rutgers.edu/~jlynch/writing⟩.

National Association of Professional Organizers
⟨http://www.napo.net⟩.

Strunk, William Jr., and E. B. White. *The Elements of Style.* 3rd ed.
New York: Macmillan, 1979. The classic—designed to help you
write more elegantly. However, it assumes that you understand
grammatical terms.

University of Maine's Links to other Writing Centers
⟨http://www.ume.maine.edu/~wcenter/others.html⟩.

Writer's Resources on the Web
⟨http//inkspot.com⟩.

HELP WITH DESIGNING ELECTRONIC DOCUMENTS

Horton, William K. *Designing and Writing Online Documentation.* 2nd
ed. New York: Wiley, 1994.

————. *Illustrating Computer Documentation.* New York: Wiley, 1991.

Lynch, Patrick J., and Sarah Horton. *Web Style Guide.* New Haven,
CT: Yale University Press, 1999. Also see their website
⟨http://info.med.yale.edu/caim/manual/contents.html⟩.

Marcus, Aaron. *Graphic Design for Electronic Documents and User
Interfaces.* New York: Addison-Wesley, 1992.

Norman, Donald A. *The Design of Everyday Things.* Cambridge: MIT,
1998.

Richman, Alan. *The WDVL: A Guide to Creating Websites.*
⟨http://www/wdvl.com/style⟩.

Tufte, Edward R. *Envisioning Information.* Cheshire, CT: Graphics,
1990.

WWWConsortium.
⟨http://www/w3.org⟩.

HELP WITH DETAILS FOR PUBLISHING AND DOCUMENTING RESEARCH

American Chemical Society. *Guide to Publishing Reports.* Washington, DC: ACS, 1983.
⟨http://www.acs.org⟩.

American Psychological Association. *Publication Manual of the American Psychological Association.* Washington, DC: APA, 1994. This manual describes the format used by publications in the natural and social sciences.
⟨http://www.apa.org⟩.

Chicago Manual of Style. 14th ed. Chicago: University of Chicago Press, 1993. The most comprehensive and definitive of the style books for publishing. Use these guidelines if you are not committed to the requirements of a particular discipline.
⟨http://www.press.uchicago.edu/Misc/Chicago/cmosfaq.html⟩.

Council of Biology Editors. *Scientific Style and Format: The CBE Manual for Authors, Editors, and Publishers.* 6th ed. Washington, DC: American Institute of Biological Sciences, 1994.
⟨www.cbe.org.cbe⟩.

Gibaldi, Joseph. *MLA Style Manual and Guide to Scholarly Publishing.* 2nd ed. New York: Modern Language Association, 1998. A guide for all the fine points for publications in foreign languages and in English literature.
⟨http://www.mla.org⟩.

HELP WITH ENGLISH AS A SECOND LANGUAGE

Allen, Edward Jay. *Advanced American Idioms.* Language Development Series, 1982.

Ammer, Christine. *American Heritage Dictionary of Idioms.* Boston: Houghton, 1997. A good and full explanation of the meaning of phrases and when to use which preposition in a phrase.

Spears, Richard A., and Linda Shinke-Llano, eds. *NTC's American Idiom Dictionary.* New York: National Textbook Company, 1993.

DICTIONARIES

American Heritage Dictionary. Contains excellent photographs and illustrations.

Merriam-Webster Dictionary
⟨http://www.m-w.com⟩.

Oxford English Dictionary (OED). 13 vols. Gives the full historical development of English words.

Roget's International Thesaurus of English Words and Phrases. 5th ed. New York: Addison Wesley, 1994. Also at ⟨http://www.thesaurus.com⟩.

A Web of Online Dictionaries. Includes foreign language dictionaries. ⟨http://www.facstaf.bucknell.edu/rbeard/diction.html⟩.

Webster's New Universal Unabridged Dictionary of the English Language. The dictionary most often cited.

To access the dictionary or thesaurus in your word-processing program, first highlight the word and then click your right mouse button.

DIRECTORIES

BigBook. Yellow pages of the Internet ⟨http://www.bigbook.com⟩.

BigFoot. A compendium of all the telephone directories in the United States. ⟨http://www.bigfoot.com⟩.

Dun's Business Locator (on CD-ROM).

Dun's Small Business Sourcing File (on CD-ROM).

Encyclopedia of Associations. Lists, with addresses, professional associations (in print and on CD-ROM).

Foundation Directory. Lists, with addresses, philanthropic foundations and foundations for specialized studies (in print and on CD-ROM).

Switchboard (white pages).
⟨http://www.switchboard.com⟩.

WhoWhere?
⟨http://www.whowhere.com/⟩.

Yahoo! People Search.
⟨http://www.yahoo.com/search/people⟩.

Yellowwweb Pages.
⟨http://www.yellowwweb.com⟩.

ENCYCLOPEDIAS

In addition to these general references, look for encyclopedias devoted to a particular subject—for example, there is a *Baseball Encyclopedia*. New York: Macmillan, 1996.

Collier's Encyclopedia. Good general information source for contemporary subjects.

Encyclopedia Americana. Good for scientific and technical topics.

Encyclopedia Britannica (in print, on CD-ROM, or online for a fee). The most definitive, comprehensive encyclopedia. Annual supplement, *Britannica Book of the Year.* Also at ⟨http://www.britannica.com⟩.

Free Internet Encyclopedia.
⟨http://clever.net/cam/encyclopedia.html⟩.

STATISTICAL SOURCES

American Statistical Index (in print and on CD-ROM). A monthly index of all U.S. government statistical publications. Also available at
⟨http://www.fedstats.gov⟩.
See also individual federal agencies' websites.

Bureau of Census Reports. Various reports, filled with all sorts of facts about American life. Based on census data collected every ten years. Some are on CD-ROM, or at
⟨http://www.census.gov⟩.

Statistical Resources on the Web
⟨http://www.lib.umich.edu/libhome/Documents.center/stats.html⟩.

QUOTATIONS ORGANIZED BY SUBJECT

Bartlett's Familiar Quotations. 16th ed. Boston: Little, Brown, 1992.
  Also available on software or at
  ⟨http://www.columbia.edu/acis/bartleby/bartlett⟩.

The Quotations Page.
  ⟨http://www.starlingtech.com/quotes⟩.

Metcalf, Fred. *The Penguin Dictionary of Modern Humorous Quotations.*
  New York: Penguin, 1988.

Oxford Dictionary of Quotations. New York: Oxford, 1997. See various
  editions on Humorous Quotations, Modern Quotations, and so
  forth.

SEARCH TOOLS FOR THE INTERNET

Subject Lists

These websites are organized as indexes; you can enter a keyword or
you can search by clicking on the topic, then subtopic, then sub-
subtopic, and so forth. The advantage is that materials have been
organized by human researchers, so most of the results will be
relevant.

About.com (each area is maintained by an expert to whom you can e-mail)	http://www.about.com
Argus Clearinghouse	http://wwwclearinghouse.net
Lycos Top 5% of the Web	http://point.lycos.com
Magellan (good subject search)	http://mckinley.com
The Mother of all Gophers (good for checking for libraries)	gopher://gopher.tc.umn.edu
Yahoo! (very fast subject search)	http://www.yahoo.com/

Metasearchers, Which Simultaneously Check for Your Terms Among Several Search Engines

If you have developed a good list of search terms, use a variety of powerful search engines—robots that search the entire Web.

Dogpile
(fun to use, it simultaneously searches twenty-five search engines)
http://www.dogpile.com

Highway 61
(very fast, it searches the six most popular search engines and arranges the results by relevance)
http://www.highway61.com

Inference Find
(also very fast and concept oriented, it searches the six top search engines and organizes the results)
http://www.inference.com/infind/

SavvySearch
(fast and thorough)
http://www.savvysearch.com

USE IT!
(a Unified Search Engine for InTernet— in Italy, includes international sites)
http://www.he.net/~kamus/useen.htm

Reference Lists and Links to Resources (Including Most Search Engines Listed Individually on Pages 211–212)

Internet browsers and library homepages provide lists with links to search engines (so you don't have to type the addresses). Alternatively, you can type the URL address for individual search engines.

The December List   http://www.december.com/cmc/info
(in addition to listing
search engines, provides
links to a variety of
helpful resources)

Internet Sleuth   http://www.isleuth.com
(includes direct links
to some databases not
on the Web)

Library of Congress   http://lcweb.loc.gov/rr/tools.html
Research Tools

Virtual Reference Desk   http://thorplus.lib.purdue.edu/
                                       reference/index.html

Powerful Search Engines

AltaVista   http://altavista.digital.com
(one of the most
comprehensive)

c/net   http://search.cnet.com

Excite   http://www.excite.com
(includes summaries,
sorted by relevance to
the topic—offering
"more like this")

HotBot   http://www.hotbot.com
(fastest and most
comprehensive; best
for complicated searches
and multimedia topics)

InfoSeek   http://www.infoseek.com
(best for simple searches;
also good for refining
searches)

Lycos
(oldest and still one of
the best although it
doesn't allow searches
for phrases)

http://www.lycos.com

NorthernLight
(provides folders for
organizing your search;
also identifies the date
of original posting—
often not given on the
website—and whether
a site is a personal page,
commercial, or
nonprofit; retrieves
documents for a fee)

http://www.northernlight.com

WebCrawler
(one of the fastest)

http://www.webcrawler.com

WorldWideWorm
(good for simple
searches)

http://www.goto.com

Search Tools for Discussion Groups and Newsgroups

To retrieve threads of conversation from previous discussions
(recommended for research purposes)

Dejanews

http://www.deja.com

Reference.com

http://www.reference.com

To find ListServs or Newsgroups by subject

*CataList: the Official
Catalog of Listserv Lists*

http://www.listserv.net/lists/
   listref.html

*Liszt, the Mailing List
Directory*

http://www.liszt.com

*Publicly Accessible
Mailing Lists*

http://www.neosoft.com/internet/
   paml

| Tile.Net/Listserv | http://www.tile.net/lists |
| FAQs for Newsgroups | http://www.smartpages.com/faqs/ |

OTHER USEFUL SITES FOR RESEARCH

US Congress on the Internet (Congressional decisions)	http://thomas.loc.gov
Environment	http://envirolink.org http://www.earthwatch.org
FAIR (Fairness and Accuracy in Reporting)	http://www.fair.org
Federal Information Network	http://www.fedworld.gov
JobWeb (job listings)	http://www.jobweb.com
Library of Congress	http://lcweb.loc.gov/
National Public Radio	http://www.npr.org
New York Public Library	http://www.nypl.org
Public Broadcasting System	http://www.pbs.org
Smithsonian Institution	http://www.si.edu
WebMuseum	http://www.netspot.unisa.edu.au/wm/
World Lecture Hall (faculty websites, organized by discipline)	http://www.utexas.edu/world/lecture/

E-Texts (Online Copies of Books, Magazines, and Newspapers)

Books, journals, and links to e-texts

| Cyberstacks | http://www.public.iastate.edu/~CYBERSTACKS |
| ElectricBook | http://www.electricbook.com |

Internet Public Library	http://ipl.sils.umich.edu
Internet Wiretap Connection	gopher://wiretap.spies.com/11/ books
Omnivore	http://way.net/omnivore/index.html
Online Books Page	http://www.cs.cmu.edu/Web/ books.html
Online Magazines	http://www.pathfinder.com
Project Bartleby	http://www.cc.columbia.edu/acis/ bartleby/index.html
Project Gutenberg	http://www.gutenberg.net
Salon	http://www.salon.com
Slate	http://www.slate.com
Wired	http://www.wired.com

Newspapers Online

(Note that most newspapers post only part of the current day's issue.)

Christian Science Monitor (complete issues since 1980)	http://www.csmonitor.com/
Los Angeles Times	http://www.latimes.com
New York Times	http://www.nytimes.com
Newsday	http://www.newsday.com
Newspapers Online (links to newspapers all over the world)	http://www.newspapers.com
Total News (links to local and national newspapers)	http://www.totalnews.com
Washington Post	http://www.washingtonpost.com

FREE E-MAIL ACCOUNTS

These accounts (paid for by advertising) have the advantage of being accessible from any computer with access to the Web. Although at times slow, they are a nice backup to accounts through work or your local library—especially when you are traveling.

Just click on the "free E-mail" button on the home page of most search engines listed on pages 211–212 or at one of these websites:

http://www.eudora.com

http://www.hotmail.com

http://www.juno.com

INDEX

ABOUT THE AUTHORS

Diana Roberts Wienbroer, Elaine Hughes, and **Jay Silverman** are the joint authors of *Rules of Thumb: A Guide for Writers,* which has sold 200,000 copies and is now available in its fourth edition, and *Rules of Thumb for Research.* They all have extensive experience teaching writing at universities across the country.